WORLD
FACTS

WORLD FACTS

GEDDES&
GROSSET

First published 1992
© 1992 Geddes & Grosset Ltd,
New Lanark, Scotland.

Cover design by Cameron Graphics Ltd,
Glasgow, Scotland.

ISBN 1 85534 089 5

Printed and bound in Great Britain.

Contents

COUNTRIES
of
THE WORLD

AFGHANISTAN

Afghanistan is a landlocked country in Southern Asia. The greater part of the country is mountainous with several peaks over 6000 metres in the central region. The climate is generally arid with great extremes of temperature. There is considerable snowfall in winter which may remain on the mountain summits the year round. The main economic activity is agriculture and although predominantly pastoral, successful cultivation takes place in the fertile plains and valleys. Natural gas is produced in northern Afghanistan and over 90% of this is piped across the border to the USSR. Other mineral resources are scattered and so far under-developed. The main exports are Karakuls (Persian lambskins), raw cotton and foodstuffs.

Area : 652 090sq km
(251 772sq mi)
Population : 15 810 000
Capital : Kabul
Other major cities : Kandahar,
Herat, Mazar-i-Sharif
Form of government :
People's Republic
Religions : Sunni Islam,
Shia Islam
Currency : Afghani

ALBANIA

Albania is a small mountainous country in the eastern Mediterranean. Its immediate neighbours are Yugoslavia and Greece, and it is bounded to the west by the Adriatic Sea. The climate is typically Mediterranean and although most rain falls in winter, severe thunderstorms frequently occur on the plain in summer. Winters are severe in the highland areas and heavy snowfalls are common. All land is state owned, with the main agricultural areas lying along the Adriatic coast and in the Korce Basin. Industry is also nationalized and output is small. The principal industries are agricultural product processing, textiles, oil products and cement. most trade is with neighbouring Yugoslavia.

Area : 28 748sq km (11 100sq mi)
Population : 3 200 000
Capital : Tirana
Other major cities : Durres,
Shkoder, Elbasan
Form of government :
Socialist Republic
Religion : Constitutionally
atheist but mainly Sunni Islam
Currency : Lek

ALGERIA

Algeria is a huge country in Northern Africa, which fringes the Mediterranean Sea in the north. Over four-fifths of Algeria is covered by the Sahara Desert to the south. Near the north coastal area the Atlas Mountains run east-west in parallel ranges. The climate in the coastal areas is warm and temperate with most of the rain falling in winter. The summers are dry and hot with temperatures rising to over 32°C. Inland beyond the Atlas Mountains conditions become more arid and temperatures range from 49°C during the day to 10°C at night. most of Algeria possesses one of the largest reserves of natural gas and oil in the world. The main exports are oil-based products, some fruit and vegetables.

Area : 2 381 741sq km
(919 590sq mi)
Population : 25 360 000
Capital : Algiers
Other major cities : Oran,
Constantine, Annaba
Form of government : Republic
Religion : Sunni Islam
Currency : Algerian dinar

ANDORRA

Situated high in the Eastern Pyrenees, the tiny state of Andorra lies between France and Spain. The state consists of deep valleys and high mountain peaks which reach heights of 3000 metres Although only 20km wide and 30km long, the spectacular scenery and climate attract many tourists. About 6 million visitors arrive each winter when the cold weather with heavy snowfalls makes for ideal skiing. In summer when the weather is mild and sunny the mountains are used for walking. Tourism and the duty-free trade are now Andorra's chief sources of income. Natives who are not involved in the tourist industry may raise sheep and cattle on the high pastures.

Area : 453sq km
(175sq mi)
Population : 51400
Capital : Andorra-Vella
Form of government :
Co-principality
Religion : RC
Currency : Franc, Peseta

ANGOLA

Situated on the Atlantic coast of West Central Africa, Angola lies about 10°S of the equator. It shares borders with Congo, Zaire, Zambia and Namibia. Its climate is tropical with temperatures constantly between 20°C and 25°C. The rainfall is heaviest in inland areas where there are vast equatorial forests. The country is also rich in minerals, however deposits of manganese, copper and phosphate are as yet unexploited. Diamonds are mined in the northeast and oil is produced near Luanda. Oil production is a most important aspect of the economy, making up about 80% of export revenue.

Area: 1 246 700sq km
(481 351sq mi)
Population : 10 020 000
Capital : Luanda
Other major cities : Huambo,
Lobito, Benguela
Form of government : People's
Republic
Religions : RC, Animist
Currency : Kwanza

ANTIGUA AND BARBUDA

Located on the eastern side of the Leeward Islands, the tiny state of Antigua and Barbuda comprises three islands _ Antigua, Barbuda and the uninhabited Redonda. Antigua's strategic position was recognized by the British in the 18th century when it was an important naval base, and later by the USA who built the island's airport during the World War II to defend the Caribbean and the Panama Canal. The climate is tropical although its average rainfall of 100mm makes it drier than most of the other islands of the West Indies. On Antigua the numerous palm-fringed sandy beaches make it an ideal tourist destination, and as a result tourism is the main industry. Barbuda is surrounded by coral reefs and the island is home to a wide range of wildlife.

Area : 440sq km (170sq mi)
Population : 85 000
Capital : St. John's
Form of government :
Constitutional monarchy
Religion : Christian
(mainly Anglican)
Currency : East Caribbean dollar

ARGENTINA

Argentina, the world's 8th largest country, stretches from the Tropic of Capricorn to Cape Horn on the southern tip of the South American continent. To the west a massive mountain chain, the Andes, forms the border with Chile. The climate ranges from warm temperate over the Pampas in the central region, to a more arid climate in the north and west, while in the extreme south conditions although also dry are much cooler. The vast fertile plains of the Pampas once provided Argentina with its main source of wealth, but as manufacturing industries were established in the early 20th century agriculture suffered badly and food exports were greatly reduced. A series of military regimes have resulted in an unstable economy which fails to provide reasonable living standards for the population.

Area : 2 766 889sq km
(1 068 296sq mi)
Population : 32 690 000
Capital : Buenos Aires
Other major cities : Cordoba,
Rosaria, Mendoza, La Plata
Form of government : Federal
Republic
Religion : RC
Currency : Austral

AUSTRALIA

Australia, the world's smallest continent, is a vast and sparsely populated island in the southern hemisphere. The most mountainous region is the Great Dividing Range which runs down the entire east coast. Because of its great size, Australia's climates range from tropical monsoon to cool temperate and also large areas of desert. Central and south Queensland are subtropical while north and central New South Wales are warm temperate. Much of Australia's wealth comes from agriculture, with huge sheep and cattle stations extending over large parts of the interior. These have helped maintain Australia's position as the world's leading producer of wool. Cereal growing is dominated by wheat.

Area : 7 686 848sq km (2 967 892sq mi)
Population : 17 100 000
Capital : Canberra
Other major cities : Sydney,
Melbourne, Brisbane, Perth,
Adelaide
Form of government : Federal
parliamentary state
Religion : Christian
Currency : Australian dollar

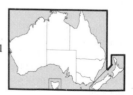

AUSTRIA

Austria is a landlocked country in central Europe and is surrounded by seven nations. The wall of mountains which runs across the centre of the country dominates the scenery. In the warm summers tourists come to walk in the forests and mountains and in the cold winters skiers come to the mountains which now boast over 50 ski resorts. Agriculture in Austria is based on small farms, many of which are run by a single family. Dairy products, beef and lamb from the hill farms contribute to exports. More then 37% of Austria is covered in forest, resulting in the paper-making industry near Graz. Unemployment is very low in Austria and its strike record has attracted multinational companies in recent years. Attachment to local customs is still strong and in rural areas men still wear lederhosen and women the traditional dirndl skirt on feast days and holidays.

Area : 83 853sq km (32 376sq mi)
Population : 7 600 000
Capital : Vienna
Other major cities : Graz,
Linz, Salzburg
Form of government :
Federal Republic
Religion : RC
Currency : Schilling

THE BAHAMAS

The Bahamas consist of an archipelago of 700 islands located in the Atlantic Ocean off the southeast coast of Florida. The largest island is Andros (4144km), and the two most populated are Grand Bahama and New Providence where the capital Nassau lies. Winters in the Bahamas are mild and summers warm. Most rain falls in May, June, September and October, and thunderstorms are frequent in summer. The islands have few natural resources, and for many years fishing and small-scale farming was the only way to make a living. Now, however, tourism, which employs over two-thirds of the workforce, is the most important industry and has been developed on a vast scale. About three million tourists, mainly from North America, visit the Bahamas each year.

Area : 13 878sq km
(5358sq mi)
Population : 256 000
Capital : Nassau
Other important city :
Freeport
Form of government :
Constitutional monarchy
Religion : Christian
Currency : Bahamian dollar

BAHRAIN

The State of Bahrain comprises 33 low-lying islands situated between the Qatar peninsula and the mainland of Saudi Arabia. Bahrain Island is the largest, and a causeway linking it to Saudi Arabia was opened in 1986. The highest point in the state is only 122.4 metres (450ft) above sea level. The climate is pleasantly warm between December and March, but very hot from June to November. Most of Bahrain is sandy and too saline to support crops but drainage schemes are now used to reduce salinity and fertile soil is imported from other islands. Oil was discovered in 1931 and revenues from oil now account for about 75% of the country's total revenue. Bahrain is being developed as a major manufacturing state, the first important enterprise being aluminium smelting. Traditional industries include pearl fishing, boat building, weaving and pottery.

Area : 678sq km (262sq mi)
Population : 486 000
Capital : Manama
Form of government : Monarchy (emirate)
Religions : Shia Islam, Sunni Islam
Currency : Bahraini dollar

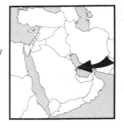

BANGLADESH

Bangladesh was formerly the Eastern Province of Pakistan. It is bounded almost entirely by India and to the south by the Bay of Bengal. The country is extremely flat and is virtually a huge delta formed by the Ganges, Brahmaputra and Meghna rivers. The country is subject to devastating floods and cyclones which sweep in from the Bay of Bengal. Most villages are built on mud platforms to keep them above water. The climate is tropical monsoon with heat, extreme humidity and heavy rainfall in the monsoon season. The short winter season is mild and dry. The combination of rainfall, sun and silt from the rivers makes the land productive, and it is often possible to grow three crops a year. Bangladesh produces about 70% of the world's jute and the production of jute-related products is a principal industry.

Area : 143 998sq km
(55 598sq mi)
Population : 113 340 000
Capital : Dhaka
Other major cities : Chittagong,
Khulna
Form of government : Republic
Religion : Sunni Islam
Currency : Taka

BARBADOS

Barbados is the most easterly island of the West Indies and lies well outside the group of islands which makes up the Lesser Antilles. Most of the island is low-lying and only in the north does it rise to over 340 metres at Mount Hillaby. The climate is tropical, but the cooling effect of the Northeast Trade winds prevents the temperatures rising above 30°C (86°F). There are only two seasons, the dry and the wet, when rainfall is very heavy. At one time the economy depended almost exclusively on the production of sugar and its by-products molasses and rum, and although the industry is now declining, sugar is still the principal export. Tourism has now taken over as the main industry and it employs 40% of the island's labour force. The island is surrounded by pink and white sandy beaches and coral reefs which are visited by almost 400 000 tourists each year.

Area : 430sq km
(166sq ml)
Population : 260 000
Capital : Bridgetown
Form of government :
Constitutional monarchy
Religions : Anglican,
Methodist
Currency : Barbados dollar

21

BELGIUM

Belgium is a relatively small country in northwest Europe with a short coastline on the North Sea. The Meuse river divides Belgium into two distinct geographical regions. To the north of the river the land slopes continuously for 150km until it reaches the North Sea where the coastlands are flat and grassy. To the south of the river is the forested plateau area of the Ardennes. Between these two regions lies the Meuse valley. Belgium is a densely populated industrial country with few natural resources. Agriculture is based on livestock production but employs only 3% of the workforce. The metal-working industry, originally based on the small mineral deposits in the Ardennes, is the most important industry, and in the northern cities new textile industries are producing carpets and clothing. Nearly all raw materials are now imported through the main port of Antwerp.

Area : 30 519sq km (11 783sq mi)
Population : 9 930 000
Capital : Brussels
Other major cities : Antwerp, Ghent, Charleroi, Liege
Form of government : Constitutional monarchy
Religion : RC
Currency : Belgium franc

BELIZE

Belize is a small Central American country located on the southeast of the Yucatan peninsula in the Caribbean Sea. Its coastline on the Gulf of Honduras is approached through some 550km of coral reefs and caya. The coastal area and north of the country are low-lying and swampy with dense forests inland. In the south the May Mountains rise to 1100 metres. The subtropical climate is warm and humid and the trade winds bring cooling sea breezes. Rainfall is heavy, particularly in the south, and hurricanes may occur in summer. The dense forests which cover most of the country provide valuable hardwoods such as mahogany. Most of the population make a living from forestry, fishing or agriculture. The main crops grown for export are sugarcane, citrus fruits (mainly grapefruit), bananas and coconuts. Industry is very underdeveloped and many people emigrate to find work.

Area : 22 965sq km (8 867sq mi)
Population : 193 000
Capital : Belmopan
Other major city :
Belize City
Form of government :
Constitutional monarchy
Religion : RC
Currency : Belize dollar

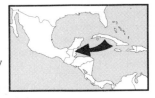

23

BENIN

Benin on the southern coast of West Africa is an ice cream cone-shaped country with a very short coastline on the Bight of Benin. The coastal area has white sandy beaches backed by lagoons and low-lying fertile lands. In the northwest the Atakora Mountains are grassy plateaux which are deeply cut into steep forested valleys. The climate in the north is tropical and in the south equatorial. There are nine rainy months each year so crops rarely fail. Farming is predominantly subsistence, with yams, cassava, maize, rice, groundnuts and vegetables forming most of the produce. The country is very poor, and lack of foreign investment prevents diversification of the economy. The main exports are palm oil, palm kernels, and cotton. Tourism is now being developed but as yet facilities for this are few except in some coastal towns.

Area : 112 622sq km
(43 483sq mi)
Population : 4 760 000
Capital : Porto-Novo
Other major cities : Contonou
Form of government : Republic
Religions : Animist, RC, Sunni Islam
Currency : Franc CFA

BERMUDA

Bermuda consists of a group of 150 small islands in the western Atlantic Ocean. It lies about 920km east of Cape Hatteras on the coast of the USA. The hilly limestone islands are the caps of ancient volcanoes rising from the sea-bed. The main island is Great Bermuda and it is linked to the other islands by bridges and causeways. The climate is pleasantly warm and humid with rain spread evenly throughout the year. Bermuda's chief agricultural products are fresh vegetables, bananas and citrus fruit. Many foreign banks and financial institutions operate from the island to take advantage of the lenient tax laws. Its proximity to the USA and the pleasant climate have led to a flourishing tourist industry.

Area : 53sq km (21sq mi)
Population : 59 066
Capital : Hamilton
Form of government :
Colony under British
administration
Religion : Protestant
Currency : Bermuda doll

BHUTAN

Surrounded by India to the south and China to the north, Bhutan rises from foothills overlooking the Brahmaputra river to the southern slopes of the Himalayas. The Himalayas, which rise to over 7 500 metres in Bhutan, make up most of the country. The climate is hot and wet on the plains but temperatures drop progressively with altitude, resulting in glaciers and permanent snow cover in the north. The valleys in the centre of the country are wide and fertile and about 95% of the workforce are farmers. Yaks reared on the high pasture land provide milk, cheese and meat. Rice is grown on the lowest ground. Vast areas of the country still remain forested as there is little demand for new farmland. Bhutan has little contact with the resat of the world and the number of visitors is limited to 1 500 each year.

Area : 47 000sq km
(18 147sq mi)
Population : 1 400 000
Capital : Thimphu
Form of government :
Constitutional monarchy
Religion : Buddhist
Currency : Ngultrum

BOLIVIA

Bolivia is a landlocked republic of central South America through which the great mountain range of the Andes runs. It is in the Andes that the highest navigable lake in the world, Lake Titicaca, is found. On the undulating depression south of the lake, the Altiplano, is the highest capital city in the world, La Paz. To the east and northeast of the mountains is a huge area of lowland containing tropical rainforests (the Lianos) and wooded savanna (the Chaco). The northeast has a heavy rainfall while in the southwest it is negligible. Temperatures vary with altitude from extremely cold on the summits to cool on the Altiplano, where at least half the population lives. Rich in natural resources, eg. oil, tin, Bolivia is not a rich country because of lack of funds for their extraction. Agriculture produces foodstuffs, sugarcane and cotton for export, and increased production of coca, from which cocaine is derived, has resulted in an illicit economy.

Area : 1 098 581sq km (424 162sq mi)
Population : 6 410 000
Capital : La Paz (administrative capital), Sucre (legal capital)
Other major city : Cochabamba
Form of government : Republic
Religion : RC
Currency : Boliviano

BOTSWANA

Botswana is a landlocked republic in Southern Africa which straddles the Tropic of Capricorn. Much of the west and southwest of the country forms part of the Kalahari desert. In the north the land is marshy around the Okavango Delta, which is home for a wide variety of wildlife. With the exception of the desert area most of the country has a subtropical climate. In winter, days are warm and nights cold while summer is hot with sporadic rainfall. The people of Botswana are mainly farmers and cattle rearing is the main activity. After independence in 1966 the exploitation of minerals started. Diamonds became an important revenue earner and the copper from the nickel/copper complex at Selebi-Pikwe was also exported. Mineral resources in the northeast are now being investigated. About 17% of the land is set aside for wildlife preservation in National Parks, Game Reserves, Game Sanctuaries and controlled hunting areas.

Area : 581 730sq km (224 606sq mi)
Population : 1 260 000
Capital : Gaborone
Other major cities : Mahalapye, Serowe, Francistown
Form of government : Republic
Religions : Animist, Anglican
Currency : Pula

BRAZIL

Brazil is a huge South American country bounded to the north, south and east by the Atlantic Ocean. It is the fifth largest country in the world and covers nearly half of the South American continent. The climate is mainly tropical however altitude, distance from the sea and prevailing winds causes many variations. In the Amazonia area it is constantly warm and humid, but in the tropical areas winters are dry and summers wet. Droughts may occur in the northeast, where it is hot and arid. About one seventh of the population is employed in agriculture and the main exported are coffee, soya bran and cocoa. Brazil is rich in minerals and is the only source of high grade quartz crystal in commercial quantities. It is also a major producer of chrome ore and it is now developing what is thought to be the richest iron ore deposits in the world.

Area : 8 511 965sq km (3 285 470sq mi)
Population : 115 600 000
Capital : Brasilia
Other major cities : Sao Paulo,
Rio de Janeiro, Salvador,
Belo Horizonte, Recife,
Porto Alegre
Form of government : Federal
Republic
Religion : RC
Currency : Cruzeiro

29

BRUNEI

The Sultanate of Brunei is located on the northwest coast of Borneo in southeast Asia. It is bounded on all sides by the Sarawak territory of Malaysia, which splits the sultanate into two separate parts. Broad tidal swamplands cover the coastal plains and inland Brunei is hilly and covered with tropical forest. The climate is tropical marine, hot and moist, with cool nights. Rainfall is heavy (2 500mm) at the coast but even heavier (5 000mm) inland. The main crops grown in Brunei are rice, vegetables and fruit, but economically the country depends primarily on its oil industry which employs 7% of the working population. Oil production began in the 1920s and now oil and natural gas account for almost all exports. Other minor products are rubber, pepper, sawn timber, gravel and animal hides.

Area : 5 765sq km
(2 226sq mi)
Population : 267 000
Capital : Bandar Seri
Begawan
Other major cities : Seria,
Kuala Belait
Form of government :
Monarchy (Sultanate)
Religion : Sunni Islam
Currency : Brunei dollar

BULGARIA

The southeast European republic of Bulgaria is located on the east Balkan peninsula and has a coast on the Black Sea. It is bounded to the north by Romania, west by Yugoslavia and south by Greece and Turkey. The centre of Bulgaria is crossed from west to east by the Balkan Mountains. The south of the country has a mediterranean climate with hot dry summers and mild winters. Further north the temperatures become more extreme and rainfall is higher in summer. Traditionally Bulgaria is an agricultural country and a revolution in farming in the 1950s has led to great increases in output. This was due to the collectivization of farms and the use of more machinery, fertilizers and irrigation. Each agricultural region now has its own specialized type of farming. Increased mechanization led to more of the workforce being available to work in mines and industry and now Bulgaria is the third most urbanized country in eastern Europe.

Area : 110 912sq km (42 823sq mi)
Population : 8 970 000
Capital : Sofia
Other major cities : Plovdiv,
Varna, Ruse, Burgas
Form of government : Republic
Religion : Eastern Orthodox
Currency : Lev

BURKINA FASO

A landlocked state in west Africa, Burkina Faso lies on the fringe of the Sahara, to the north. The country is made up of vast monotonous plains and low hills which rise to 700 metres in the southwest. Precipitation is generally low, the heaviest rain falling in the southwest, while the rest of the country is semi-desert. The dusty grey plains in the north and west have infertile soils which have been further impoverished by overgrazing and overcultivation. About 90% of the people live by farming, and food crops include sorghum, beans and maize. Some cotton, livestock and oil seeds are exported. There is a great shortage of work and many of the younger population go to Ghana and Cote d'Ivoire for employment. The only main industries are textiles and metal products.

Area : 274 200sq km
(105 869sq mi)
Population : 8 760 000
Capital : Ouagadougou
Form of government : State
Religions : Animist,
Sunni Islam
Currency : Franc CFA

BURMA (MYANMAR)

The union of Myanmar (formerly Burma) is the second largest country in southeast Asia. The heartland of the country is the valley of the Irrawaddy. The north and west of the country are mountainous and in the east the Shan Plateau runs along the border with Thailand. The climate is equatorial at the coast, changing to tropical monsoon over most of the interior. The Irrawaddy river flows into the Andaman Sea, forming a huge delta area which is ideal land for rice cultivation. Rice is the country's staple food and accounts for half the country's export earnings. Burma is rich in timber and minerals but because of poor communications, lack of development and unrest among the ethnic groups, the resources have not been fully exploited.

Area : 676 578sq km (261 227sq mi)
Population : 39 300 000
Capital : Yangon
(formerly Rangoon)
Other major cities :
Mandalay,
Moulmein, Pegu
Form of government :
Republic
Religion : Buddhist
Currency : Kyat

BURUNDI

Burundi is a small densely populated country in central east Africa, bounded by Rwanda to the north, Tanzania to the east and south and Zaire to the west. It has a very mountainous terrain, with much of the country above 1 500 metres. The climate is equatorial but modified by altitude. The savanna in the east is several degrees hotter than the plateau and there are two wet seasons. The soils are not rich but there is enough rain to grow crops in most areas. The main food crops are bananas, sweet potatoes, peas, lentils and beans. Cassava is grown near the shores of Lake Tanganyika. The main cash crop is coffee and this accounts for 90% of Burundi's export earnings. There is a little commercial fishing on Lake Tanganyika, otherwise industry is very basic.

Area : 27 834sq km
(10 747sq mi)
Population : 5 540 000
Capital : Bujumbura
Form of government : Republic
Religion : RC
Currency : Burundi franc

CAMBODIA

The southeast Asian state of Cambodia is bounded by Thailand, Laos and Vietnam and its southern coast lies on the Gulf of Thailand. The heart of the country is saucer-shaped and gently rolling alluvial plains are drained by the Mekong river. The Dangrek Mountains form the frontier with Thailand in the northwest. In general Cambodia has a tropical Monsoon climate and about half of the land is tropical forest. During the rainy season the Mekong swells and backs into the Great Lake (Tonle Sap), increasing its size threefold. Almost 162 000 hectares of land are flooded by this seasonal rise of the Mekong and this area is left with rich silt when the river recedes. Crop production depends entirely on the rainfall and floods but production was badly disrupted during the civil war and yields still remain low. Industry, also, has not recovered from the ravages of war.

Area : 181 035sq km (69 898sq mi)
Population : 8 300 000
Capital : Phnom Penh
Other major cities : Kampong
Cham, Battambang
Form of government :
People's Republic
Religion : Buddhist
Currency : Riel

CAMEROON

The triangular republic of Cameroon is a country of diverse landscapes in west central Africa. It stretches from Lake Chad at its apex to the northern borders of Equatorial Guinea, Gabon and the Congo in the south. The landscape ranges from low-lying lands, through the semi-desert Sahel, to dramatic mountain peaks and then to the grassy savanna, rolling uplands, steaming tropical forests and hardwood plantation. Further south are the volcanoes, including Mount Cameroon, and the palm beaches at Kribi and Limbe. The climate is equatorial with high temperatures and plentiful rain. The majority of the population lives in the south where they grow maize and vegetables. In the drier north where drought and hunger are well known, life is harder. Bananas, coffee and cocoa are the major exports although oil, gas and aluminium are becoming increasingly important.

Area : 475 442sq km
(183 568sq mi)
Population : 11 540 000
Capital : Yaounde
Other major city : Doula
Form of government : Republic
Religions : Animist, RC, Sunni
Islam
Currency : Franc CFA

CANADA

The second largest country in the world, and the largest in north America, Canada is a land of great climatic and geographical extremes. It lies to the north of the USA and has both Pacific and Atlantic coasts. The Rocky Mountains and Coast Mountains run down the west side and the highest point, Mount Waddington (4042m), is in British Columbia. Climates, from polar conditions in the north, to cool temperate in the south with considerable differences from west to east. More than 80% of its farmland is in the prairies that stretch from Alberta to Manitoba. Wheat and grain crops cover three-quarters of the arable land. Canada is rich in forest reserves which cover more than half of the total land area. The most valuable minerals deposits (oil, gas, coal and iron ore) are found in Alberta. Most industry in Canada is associated with processing its natural resources.

Area : 9 976 139sq km (3 851 787sq mi)
Population : 26 600 000
Capital : Ottawa
Other major cities : Toronto,
Montreal, Vancouver, Quebec
Form of government : Federal
parliamentary state
Religions : RC, United Church
of Canada, Anglican
Currency : Canadian dollar

CAPE VERDE

Cape Verde, one of the world's smallest nations is situated in the Atlantic Ocean, about 620km northwest of Senegal. It consists of 10 islands and 5 islets. The islands are divided into the Windward group and the Leeward group. Over 50% of the population live on Sao Tiago on which is Praia the capital. The climate is arid with a cool dry season from December to June and warm dry conditions for the rest of the year. Rainfall is sparse and the islands suffer from periods of severe drought. Agriculture is mostly confined to irrigated inland valleys and the chief crops are coconuts, sugar cane, potatoes and cassava. Bananas and some coffee are grown for export. Fishing for tuna and lobsters is an important industry but in general the economy is shaky and Cape Verde relies heavily on foreign aid.

Area : 4 033sq km
(240 534sq mi)
Population : 369 000
Capital : Praia
Form of government : Republic
Religion : RC
Currency : Cape Verde escudo

CENTRAL AFRICAN REPUBLIC

The Central African Republic is a landlocked country in central Africa bordered by Chad in the north, Cameroon in the west, Sudan in the east and the Congo in the south. The terrain consists of a 610m-915m high undulating plateau with dense tropical forest in the south and a semi-desert area in the east. The climate is tropical with little variation in temperature. The wet months are May, June, October and November. Most of the population live in the west and in the hot, humid south and southwest . Over 86% of the working population are subsistence farmers and the main crops grown are cassava, groundnuts, bananas, plantains, millet and maize. Livestock rearing is small-scale because of the prevalence of the disease-carrying tsetse fly. Gems and industrial diamonds are mined and vast deposits of uranium have been discovered.

Area : 622 984sq km
(240 534sq mi)
Population : 2 900 000
Capital : Bangui
Form of government : Republic
Religions : Animist, RC
Currency : Franc CFA

CHAD

Chad, a landlocked country in the centre of northern Africa, extends from the edge of the equatorial forests in the south to the middle of the Sahara desert in the north. It lies more than 1 600km from the nearest coast. The climate is tropical with adequate rainfall in the south but the north experiences semi-desert conditions. In the far north of the country the Tibesti Mountains rise from the desert sand more than 3 000 metres. The southern part of Chad is the most densely populated and its relatively well-watered savanna has always been the country's most arable region. Recently, however, even here the rains have failed. Normally this area is farmed for cotton (the main cash crop), millet, sorghum, groundnuts, rice and vegetables. Fishing is carried out in the rivers and in Lake Chad. Cotton ginning is the principal industry.

Area : 1 284 000sq km
(495 752sq mi)
Population : 5 540 000
Capital : N'Djamena
Other major cities : Sarh,
 Moundou
Form of government : Republic
Religions : Sunni Islam,
Animist
Currency : Franc CFA

40

CHILE

Chile lies like a backbone down the Pacific coast of the South American continent. Its Pacific coastline is 4 200km long. Because of its enormous range in latitude it has almost every kind of climate from desert conditions to icy wastes. The north, in which lies the Atacama desert, is extremely arid while the central region is mediterranean and the south cool temperate. 60% of the population live in the central valley where the climate is similar to southern California. The land here is fertile and the principal crops grown are wheat, sugar beet, maize and potatoes. It is also in the central valley that the vast copper mine of El Teniente is located. This is one of the largest copper mines in the world and accounts for Chile's most important source of foreign exchange.

Area : 756 945sq km (292 256sq mi)
Population : 12 960 000
Capital : Santiago
Other major cities : Vina del Mar, Talcahuano, Arica
Form of government : Republic
Religion : RC
Currency : Chilean peao

CHINA

China, the third largest country in the world, covers a large area of east Asia. In western China most of the terrain is very inhospitable— in the northwest there are deserts which extend into Mongolia and the USSR, and much of the southwest consists of the ice -capped peaks of Tibet. The southeast has a green and well watered landscape comprising terraced hillsides and paddy fields. Most of China has a temperate climate but in such a large country wide ranges of latitude and altitudes produce local variations. It is an agricultural country, and intensive cultivation and horticulture is necessary to feed its large population. Since the death of Mao in 1976 China has experienced a huge modernisation of agriculture and industry supplied by expertise, capital and technology from Japan and the West. The country has also been opened up to tourists.

Area : 9 596 961sq km
(3 705 387sq mi)
Population : 1 114 000 000
Capital : Beijing (Peking)
Other major cities : Shanghai,
Tianjin, , Wuhan, , Chengdu
Form of government : People's
republic
Religions : Buddhist, Taoist,
Confucianism
Currency : Yuan

COLOMBIA

Colombia is situated in the north of South America and most of the country lies between the equator and 10 north. The Andes, which split into three ranges (the Cordilleras) in Colombia, run north along the west coast and gradually disappear towards the Caribbean Sea. Half of Colombia lies east of the Andes and much of this region is covered in tropical grassland. Towards the Amazon Basin the vegetation changes to tropical forest. The climates in Colombia include equatorial and tropical according to altitude. Very little of the country is under cultivation although much of the soil is fertile. The range of climates result in an extraordinary variety of crops of which coffee is the most important. Colombia is rich in minerals and produces about half of the world's emeralds. It is south America's leading producer of coal and oil has recently been discovered.

Area : 1 138 914sq km
(439 735sq mi)
Population : 33 000 000
Capital : Bogota
Other major cities : Medellin,
Cali, Barranquilla, Cartagena
Form of government : Republic
Religion : RC
Currency : Peao

COMMONWEALTH OF INDEPENDENT STATES (C.I.S)

An organization created in 1991 to represent the common interests of the independent states of the former U.S.S.R. There are eleven member states.

Armenia that part of Armenia which forms the Republic of Armenia. The capital is Yerevan. (Pop. 3 267 000)

Azerbaidzhan a former republic of the U.S.S.R, which declared its independence in 1991. It borders Azerbaijan in Iran and the Caspian Sea. The capital is Baku. (Pop. 6 506 000)

Belorussia a former republic of the U.S.S.R. which declared itself independent in 1990. It borders Poland on its western side, and lies to the south of Latvia and Lithuania. The capital is Minsk. (Pop. 9 878 000)

Georgia a former republic in the south-west of the U.S.S.R., situated in the Caucasus. It declared itself independent in 1991. The capital is Tbilisi. (Pop. 5 976 000)

Kazakhstan a former republic of the U.S.S.R., lying in the central southern region between the Caspian Sea and China. It declared sovereignty in 1990. The capital is Almaata. (Pop. 15 654 000)

Kirghizia a former republic of south central U.S.S.R. on the border with China. It declared itself independent in 1990. The capital is Fruze. (Pop. 3 886 000)

Moldavia a republic which declared its independence from the U.S.S.R. in 1991. It lies between Romania and the Ukraine. The capital is Kishinev. (Pop. 971 000)

Russian Federation the largest of the fifteen former constituent republics of the U.S.S.R., which declared sovereignty in 1991. It is a vast country, which also includes 17 autonomous republics, such as Checheningush and Dagestan. Towards the west, the Ural Mountains run from north to south and these form a theoretical border between Europe (to the west) and Asia (to the east). Most of the population live in the European section, as the eastern part, which stretches across the whole of northern Asia to the Pacific, is largely covered by the wilderness of Siberia. The northern coast is on the Arctic Ocean, but there are other shores on the Baltic Sea to the west, and the Caspian and Black Seas to the south-east. An industrial nation, Russia has extensive reserves of oil, gas, gold, coal and iron. The main language is Russian, although many other languages are spoken. The capital is Moscow. (17 075 400 sq km/6 592 800 sq mi; pop. 142 117 000; cur. Rouble = 100kopeks)

Tadzhikistan a former republic of southern central U.S.S.R., occupying the mountainous region on the border with China and Afghanistan. It declared independence in 1991. The capital is Dushanube. (Pop. 5 100 000)

Turkmenistan a former republic in the south if the U.S.S.R. bordering Afghanistan and Iran, and with a shoreline on the Caspian Sea. It declared sovereignty in 1990. The capital is Ashkhabad. (Pop. 3 600 000)

Ukraine formerly the western-most republic of the U.S.S.R., bordering Romania and Poland; it declared itself independent in August 1991. The capital is Kiev. (Pop. 51 700 000)

Uzbekistan a former republic of south-central U.S.S.R., to the north of Turkmenistan. It declared sovereignty in 1990. The capital is Tashkent. (Pop. 20 300 000)

COMOROS

The Comoros consist of three volcanic islands in the Indian Ocean situated between mainland Africa and Madagascar. Physically four islands make up the group but the island of Mayotte remained a French dependency when the three western islands became a federal Islamic republic in 1975. The islands are mostly forested and the tropical climate is affected by Indian monsoon winds from the north. There is a wet season from November to April. Only small areas of the islands are cultivated and most of this land belongs to foreign plantation owners. The chief product was formerly sugar cane, but now vanilla, copra, maize, cloves and essential oils are the most important products. The forests provide timber for building and there is a small fishing industry.

Area : 2 235sq km (863sq mi)
Population : 503 000
Capital : Moroni
Form of government : Federal Islamic republic
Religion : Sunni Islam
Currency : Comorian franc

CONGO

Formerly a French colony, the Republic of the Congo is situated in west central Africa where it straddles the equator. The climate is equatorial, with a moderate rainfall and a small range of temperature. The Bateke Plateau has a long dry season but the Congo Basin is more humid and rainfall approaches 2 500mm each year. About 62% of the total land area is covered with equatorial forest from which timbers such as Okoume and sapele are produced. Valuable hardwoods such as mahogany are exported. Cash crops such as coffee and cocoa are mainly grown on large plantations but food crops are grown on small farms usually worked by the women. A manufacturing industry is now growing and oil discovered off shore accounts for most of the Congo's revenues.

Area : 342 000sq km
(132 046sq mi)
Population : 2 260 000
Capital : Brazzaville
Other major city : Pointe-Noire
Form of government : Republic
Religion : RC
Currency : Franc CFA

COSTA RICA

With the Pacific Ocean to the south and west and the Caribbean Sea to the east, Costa Rica is sandwiched between the central American countries of Nicaragua and Panama. Much of the country consists of volcanic mountain chains which run northwest to south east. The climate is tropical with a small temperature range and abundant rain. The dry season is from December to April. The most populated area is the Valle Central which was first settled by the Spanish in the 16th century. The upland areas have rich volcanic soils which are good for coffee growing and the slopes provide lush pastures for cattle. Coffee and bananas are grown commercially and are the major agricultural exports. Costa Rica's mountainous terrain provides hydro electric power which makes almost self sufficient in electricity, and attractive scenery for its growing tourist industry.

Area : 51 100sq km
(19 730sq mi)
Population : 2 910 000
Capital : San Jose
Other major city : Limon
Form of government :
Republic
Religion : RC
Currency : Costa Rican colon

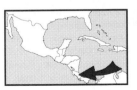

COTE D'IVOIRE

A former French colony in west Africa, Cote d'Ivoire is located on the Gulf of Guinea with Ghana to the east and Liberia to the west. The southwest coast has rocky cliffs but further east there are coastal plains which are the country's most prosperous region. The climate is tropical and affected by distance from the sea. The coastal area has two wet seasons but in the north, there is only the one. Cote d'Ivoire is basically an agricultural country which produces cocoa, coffee, rubber, bananas and pineapples. It is the world's largest producer of cocoa and the fourth largest producer of coffee. These two crops bring in half the country's export revenue. Since independence industrialisation has developed rapidly particularly food processing, textiles and sawmills.

Area : 322 463sq km
(124 503sq mi)
Population : 12 100 000
Capital : Yamoussoukro
Other major cities : Abidjan,
Bouake, Daloa
Form of government : Republic
Religions : Animist, Sunni
Islam, RC
Currency : Franc CFA

50

CUBA

Cuba is the largest and most westerly of the Greater Antilles group of islands in the West Indies. It is strategically positioned at the entrance of the Gulf of Mexico and lies about 140km south off the tip of Florida. Cuba is as big as all other Caribbean islands put together and is home to a third of the whole West Indian population. The climate is warm and generally rainy and hurricanes are liable to occur between June and November. The island consists mainly of extensive plains and the soil is fertile. The most important agricultural product is sugar and its- by products, and the processing of these is the most important industry. Most of Cuba's trade is with other communist countries particularly the USSR.

Area : 110 861sq km
(42 803sq mi)
Population : 10 580 000
Capital : Havana
Other major cities :
Santiago de Cuba,
Camaguey, HoIguin
Form of government : Socialist republic
Religion : RC
Currency : Cuban peso

CYPRUS

Cyprus is an island which lies in the eastern Mediterranean about 85km south of Turkey. It has a long thin panhandle and is divided from west to east by two parallel ranges of mountains which are separated by a wide central plain open to the sea at either end. The highest point is Mount Olympus (1951m) in the southwest. The climate is Mediterranean with very hot dry summers and warm damp winters. This contributes towards the great variety of crops grown e.g. early potatoes, vegetables cereals, tobacco, olives, bananas, and grapes. The grapes are used for the strong wines and sherries for which Cyprus is famous. Fishing is a significant industry but above all the island depends on visitors and it is the tourist industry which has led to a recovery in the economy since 1974.

Area : 9 251sq km (3 572sq mi)
Population : 698 800
Capital : Nicosia
Other major cities : Limassol, Larnaca
Form of government : Republic
Religions : Greek orthodox, Sunni Islam
Currency : Cyprus pound

CZECHOSLOVAKIA

Czechoslovakia is landlocked at the heart of central Europe. It is bounded by Germany, Poland, USSR, Hungary and Austria. Natural boundaries are formed by the Carpathian and Sudeten Mountains in the north and the river Danube in the south. The climate is humid continental with warm summers and cold winters. Most rain falls in summer and thunderstorms are frequent. Agriculture, although accounting for only a small percentage of the national income, is highly developed and efficient. Major crops are sugar beet, wheat and potatoes. Over a third of the labour force is employed in industry, the most important being iron and steel, coal, machinery, cement and paper. Recently investment has gone into electronic factories and research establishments.

Area : 127 876sq km
(49 373sq mi)
Population : 15 620 000
Capital : Prague
Other major cities : Bratislava,
Brno, Ostrava, Kosice
Form of government : Federal
republic
Religions : RC, Protestant
Currency : Koruna

DENMARK

Denmark is a small European state lying between the North Sea and the entrance to the Baltic. It consists of a western peninsula and an eastern archipelago of 406 islands only 89 of which are populated. The country is very low lying and the proximity of the sea combined with the effect of the Gulf Stream result in warm sunny summers and cold cloudy winters. The scenery is very flat and monotonous but the soils are good and a wide variety of crops can be grown. It is an agricultural country and three-quarters of the land is cultivated mostly by the rotation of grass, barley, oats and sugar beet. Animal husbandry is however the most important activity, its produce include the famous bacon and butter. Despite Denmark's limited range of raw materials it produces a wide range of manufactured goods and is famous for its imaginative design of furniture, silverware and porcelain.

Area : 4 3077sq km (16 632sq mi)
Population : 5 140 000
Capital : Copenhagen
Other major cities : Aarhus,
Odense, Aalborg
Form of government :
Constitutional monarchy
Religion : Lutheran
Currency : Danish krone

DJIBOUTI

Djibouti is situated in northeast Africa and is bounded almost entirely by Ethiopia except in the southeast where it shares a border with Somalia. Its coastline is on the Gulf of Aden. The land which is mainly basalt plains has some mountains rising to over 1 500m. The climate is hot, among the world's hottest, and extremely dry. Only a tenth of the land can be farmed even for grazing so it has great difficulty supporting its modest population of 484 000. The native population are mostly nomadic, moving from oasis to oasis or across the border to Ethiopia in search of grazing land. Most food stuffs for the urban population in Djibouti city are imported. Cattle, hides and skins are the main exports.

Area : 23 200sq km (8 958sq mi)
Population : 484 000
Capital : Djibouti
Form of government : Republic
Religion : Sunni Islam
Currency : Djibouti franc

DOMINICA

Discovered by Columbus, Dominica is the most northerly of the Windward Islands in the West Indies. It is situated between the islands of Martinique and Guadeloupe. The island is very rugged and with the exception of 225sq km of flat land, it consists of three inactive volcanoes, the highest of which is 1 447m. The climate is tropical and even on the leeward coast it rains two days out of three. The wettest season is from June to October when hurricanes often occur. The steep slopes are difficult to farm but agriculture provides almost all Dominica's exports. Bananas are the main agricultural export but copra, citrus fruits, cocoa, bay leaves and vanilla are also revenue earners. Industry is mostly based on the processing of the agricultural products.

Area : 751sq km (290sq mi)
Population : 81 200
Capital : Rosseau
Form of government : Republic
Religion : RC
Currency : Franc

DOMINICAN REPUBLIC

The Dominican Republic forms the eastern portion of the island of Hispaniola in the West Indies. It covers two-thirds of the island, the smaller portion consisting of Haiti. The west of the country is made up of four almost parallel mountain ranges and between the two most northerly is the fertile Cibao valley. The southeast is made up of fertile plains. Although well endowed with fertile land, only about 30% is cultivated. Sugar is the main crop and mainstay of the country's economy. It is grown mainly on plantations in the southeast plains. Other crops grown are coffee, cocoa and tobacco. Some mining of gold, silver, platinum, nickel and aluminium is carried out but the main industries are food processing and making consumer goods. The island has fine beaches and tourism is developing fast.

Area : 48 734sq km
(18 816sq mi)
Population : 7 200 000
Capital : Santo Domingo
Other major city :
Santiago de los Caballeros
Form of government :
Republic
Currency : Dominican peso

ECUADOR

Situated in northwest of the South American continent, Ecuador is bounded to the north by Colombia and to the east and south by Peru. The country contains over thirty active volcanos. Running down the middle of Ecuador are two ranges of the Andes which are divided by a central plateau. The coastal area consists of plains and the eastern area is made up of tropical jungles. The climate varies from equatorial through warm temperate to mountain conditions according to altitude. It is in the coastal plains that plantations of bananas, cocoa, coffee and sugar cane are found. In contrast to this the highland areas are adapted to grazing, dairying and cereal growing. The fishing industry is important on the Pacific Coast and processed fish is one of the main exports. Oil is produced in the eastern region and crude oil is Ecuador's most important export.

Area : 283 561sq km
(109 483sq mi)
Population : 10 490 000
Capital : Quito
Other major cities : Guayaquil,
Cuenca
Form of government : Republic
Currency : Sucre

EGYPT

Situated in northeast Africa, Egypt is the doorway between Africa and Asia. Its outstanding physical feature is the river Nile, the valley and delta of which covers about 35 580sq km. The climate is mainly dry but there are winter rains along the Mediterranean coast. The temperatures are comfortable in winter but summer temperatures are extremely high particularly in the south. The rich soils deposited by floodwaters along the banks of the Nile can support a large population and the delta is one of the world's most fertile agricultural regions. 96% of the population live in the delta and Nile valley where the main crops are rice, cotton, sugar cane, maize, tomatoes and wheat. The main industries are food processing and textiles. The economy has been boosted by the discovery of oil and although not in large quantities it is enough to supply Egypt's needs and leave surplus for export.

Area : 1 001 449sq km
(386 659sq mi)
Population : 50 740 000
Capital : Cairo
Other major cities : Alexandria,
El Giza
Form of government : Republic
Religions : Sunni Islam, Christian
Currency : Egyptian pound

EL SALVADOR

El Salvador is the smallest and most densely populated state in Central America. It is bounded north and east by Honduras and has a pacific coast to the south. Two volcanic ranges run from east to west across the country. The Lempa river cuts the southern ranges in the centre of the country and opens as a large sandy delta to the Pacific Ocean. Although fairly near to the equator, the climate tends to be warm rather than hot and the highlands have a cooler temperate climate. The country is predominantly agricultural and 32% of the land is used for crops such as coffee, cotton, maize, beans, rice and sorghum, and a slightly smaller area is used for grazing cattle, pigs, sheep and goats. A few industries such as food processing, textiles and chemicals are found in the major towns.

Area : 21 041sq km
(8 123sq mi)
Population : 5 210 000
Capital : San Salvador
Other major cities :
Santa Ana, San Miguel
Form of government :
Republic
Religion : RC
Currency : Colón

EQUATORIAL GUINEA

Equatorial Guinea lies about 200km north of the equator on the hot humid coast of west Africa. The country consists of asquare shaped mainland area (Mbini) with its few small offshore islets, and the islands of Bioko and Pagalu. The climate is tropical and the wet season in Bioko and Pegalu lasts from December to February. Bioko is a very fertile volcanic island and it is here the capital Malabo is sited beside a volcanic crater flooded by the sea. It is also the centre of the country's cocoa production and the country now relies heavily on foreign aid. There is however much potential for a tourist industry.

Area : 28 051sq km
(10830sq mi)
Population : 417 000
Capital : Malabo
Other major city : Bata
Form of government :
Republic
Religion : RC
Currency : Franc CFA

ESTONIA

Estonia lies to the northwest of the USSR and is bounded to the north by the Gulf of Finland, to the west by the Baltic sea and to the south by Latvia. It is the smallest of the three previous Soviet Baltic Republics. Agriculture and dairy farming are the chief occupations and there are nearly three hundred agricultural collectives and state farms. The main products are grain, potatoes, vegetables, meat, milk and eggs. Livestock includes cattle, sheep, goats and pigs. Almost 22% of Estonia is forested and this provides material for sawmills, furniture, match and pulp industries. The country has rich, high quality shale deposits and phosphorous has been found near Tallinin. Peat deposits are substantial and supply some of the electric power stations.

Area : 45 100sq km
(17 413sq mi)
Population : 1 573 000
Capital : Tallinin
Other major city :
Tartu, Narva
Form of government :
Republic
Religion : Orthodox, Lutheran
Currency : Ruble

ETHIOPIA

Ethiopia, one of Africa's largest countries, stretches from the shores of the Red Sea to the north of Kenya. Most of the country is highlands which drops sharply towards Sudan in the west and the Red Sea in the northeast. The wide range of latitudes Ethiopia has, means climatic variations between the high temperate plateau and the hot humid lowlands. The country is very vulnerable to drought but in some areas thunderstorms can erode soil from the slopes reducing the area available for crop planting. Coffee is the main source of rural income and teff is the main food grain. The droughts in 1989-90 have brought much famine. Employment outside agriculture is confined to a small manufacturing sector in Addis Ababa and Asmara. The country is wrecked with environmental, economic and political problems and many of the population have trekked into Sudan as refugees.

Area : 1 221 900sq km (471 776sq mi)
Population : 50 000 000
Capital : Addis Ababa
Other major city : Asmara, Dire Dawa
Form of government : People's
republic
Religion : Sunni Islam,
Ethiopian orthodox
Currency : Ethiopian birr

63

FIJI

Fiji is one of the largest nations in the western Pacific and consists of some 320 islands and atolls, but only 150 are inhabited. It is situated around the 180° International Date Line and lies about 17° south of the equator. Fiji has high rainfall, high temperatures and plenty of sunshine all year round. The two main islands Viti Levu and Vanua Levu are extinct volcanoes and most of the islands in the group are fringed with coral reefs. The southeast of the islands have tropical rain forests but a lot of timber has been felled and soil erosion is a growing problem. The main cash crop is sugar cane although copra, ginger and fish are also exported. Tourism is now a major industry.

Area : 18 274sq km
(7056sq mi)
Population : 727 104
Capital : Suva
Form of government :
Republic
Religion :Christian, Hindu
Currency : Fiji dollar

FINLAND

Finland lies at the eastern limit of western Europe with the USSR to the east and the Gulf of Boltnia to the west. Most of the country is low lying except for the north which rises to over 1000m in Lapland. It is covered with extensive forests and thousands of lakes. The climate has great extremes between summer and winter. Winter is very severe and lasts about six months. Even in the south snow covers the ground for three months in winter. Summers are short but quite warm with light rain throughout the country. Finland is largely self-sufficient in food and produces great surpluses of dairy produce. Most crops are grown in the southwest . In the north reindeer are herded and forests yeild great quantities of timber for export. Major industries are timber products, wood pulp and paper, machinery and shipbuilding, which has developed due to the country's great need for an efficient fleet of ice breakers.

Area : 338 127sq km (130 551sq mi)
Population : 4 970 000
Capital : Helsinki
Other major city : Turku,
Tampere
Form of government : Republic
Religion : Lutheran
Currency : Markka

FRANCE

France is the largest country in Europe outside the USSR and has a coastline on the English Channel, the Mediterranean Sea and on the Atlantic Ocean. The lowest parts of the country are the great basins of the north and southwest from which it rises to the Massy Central and the higher Alps, Jura and Pyrénées. Climate ranges from moderate maritime in the northwest to Mediterannean in the south. Farming is possible in all parts of France. The western shores are ideal for rearing livestock, while the Paris Basin is good arable land. It is in the southwest around Bordeaux that the vineyards produce some of the world's best wines. The main industrial area of France is in the north and east, and the main industries are iron and steel engineering, chemicals, textiles and electrical goods.

Area : 551 500sq km
(212 934sq mi)
Population : 56 180 000
Capital : Paris
Other major city : Lyon,
Marseille, , Bordeaux, Toulouse
Form of government : Republic
Religion : RC
Currency : Franc

GABON

Gabon is a small country in west central Africa which straddles the equator. It has a low narrow coastal plain and the rest of the country comprises a low plateau. Three-quarters of Gabon is covered with dense tropical forest. The climate is hot, humid and typically equatorial with little or no seasonal variations. Until the 1960s timber was virtually Gabon's only resource and then oil was discovered. By the mid 1980s it was Africa's sixth largest oil producer and other minerals such as manganese, uranium and iron ore were being exploited. Much of the earnings from these resources weresquandered and most of the Gabonese people remain subsistence farmers. The country has great tourist potential but because of the dense hardwood forests transport links with the interior are very difficult.

Area : 267 667sq km
(103 346sq mi)
Population : 1 220 000
Capital : Libreville
Other major city : Port Gentile
Form of government : Republic
Religion : RC, Animist
Currency : Franc CFA

THE GAMBIA

Gambia, the smallest country in Africa, pokes like a crooked finger into Senegal. The country is divided along its entire length by the river Gambia which can only be crossed at two main ferry crossings. The Gambia has two very different seasons. In the dry season there is little rainfall, then the southwest monsoon sets in with spectacular storms producing heavy rain for four months. Most Gambians live in villages with a few animals, and grow enough millet and sorghum to feed themselves. Groundnuts are the main and only export crop of any significance. The river provides a thriving local fishing industry and on the white sandy beaches on the coast are becoming increasingly popular with foreign tourists.

Area : 11 295sq km
(4 361sq mi)
Population : 875 000
Capital : Banjul
Form of government :
Republic
Religion : Sunni Islam
Currency : Dalasi

GERMANY

Germany is a large country in northern central Europe which comprises the former East and West German republics. In the north is the North German Plain which merges with the North Rhinelands in the west. Further south, a plateau which stretches across the country from east to west, is divided by the river Rhine. In the southwest the Black Forest separates the Rhine Valley from the fertile valleys and scarplands of the Swabia. The bohemian Uplands and Erz Mountains mark the border with Czechoslovakia. Generally the country has warm summers and cold winters. Agricultural products include wheat, rye, barley, oats, potatoes and sugar beet. The main industrial and most densely populated areas are in the Rhur Valley. Principal industries are mechanical and electrical engineering. Chemical and textile industries are found along the Rhine and motor vehicle industry in the large provincial cities. The country depends heavily on imports.

Area : 356 910sq km (137 803sq mi)
Population : 79 070 000
Capital : Berlin, Bonn (Seat of government)
Other major cities : Hamburg,
Munich, Frankfurt, Leipzig
Form of government : Republic
Religions : Lutheran, RC
Currency : Deutsche mark

GHANA

Ghana is located on the southern coast of west Africa between Côte d'Ivoire and Togo. It has palm fringed beaches of white sand along the Gulf of Guinea and where the great river Volta meets the sea there are peaceful blue lagoons. The climate on the coast is equatorial and towards the north there are steamy tropical evergreen forests which give way in the far north to tropical savanna. The landscape becomes harsh and barren near the border with Burkina Faso. Most Ghanaians are village dwellers whose homes are made of locally available materials. The south of the country has been most exposed to European influence and it is here that cocoa, rubber, palm oil and coffee are grown. Ghana has important mineral resources such as manganese and bauxite. Most of Ghana's towns are in the south but rapid growth has turned many of them into unplanned sprawls.

Area : 238 533sq km
(92 098sq mi)
Population : 14 900 000
Capital : Accra
Other major city : Kumasi,
Tamale, Sekondi-Takoradi
Form of government : Republic
Religion : Protestant, Animist, RC
Currency : Cedi

GREECE

The Greek peninsula is the most south easterly extension of Europe. The Pindus Mountains divide Greece from the Albanian border in the north to the Gulf of Corinth in the south. About 70% of the land is hilly with harsh mountain climates and poor soils. The Greek islands and coastal regions have a typical Mediterranean climate with mild rainy winters and hot dry summers. Winter in the northern mountains is severe with deep snow and heavy precipitation. Agriculture is the chief activity and large scale farming is concentrated on the east coasts. The main industries are small processing plants for tobacco, food and leather. Fishing is an important activity around the 2000 islands which lie off the mainland. Tourists visit the country in the summer for the sun and in winter for its spectacular ancient ruins.

Area : 131 990sq km (50 961sq mi)
Population : 10 140 000
Capital : Athens
Other major city :Thessaloníki,
Piraeus, Patras
Form of government : Republic
Religion : Greek orthodox
Currency : Drachma

71

GRENADA

Grenada is the most southerly of the Windward Island chain in the Caribbean. Its territory includes the southern Grenadine Islands to the north. The main islands consists of the remains of extinct volcanoes and has an attractive wooded landscape. In the dry season its typical climate is very pleasant with warm days and cool nights but in the wet season it is hot day and night. Agriculture is the islands main industry and the chief crops grown for export are cocoa, nutmegs, bananas and mace. Apart from the processing of its crops Grenada has little manufacturing industry although tourism is an important source of foreign revenue. It is a popular port of call for cruise ships.

Area : 344sq km (133sq mi)
Population : 110 000
Capital : St. Georges
Form of government :
Constitutional monarchy
Religion : RC, Anglican,
Methodist
Currency : East Caribbean
dollar

GUATEMALA

Guatemala is situated between the Pacific Ocean and the Caribbean Sea where North America meets Central America. It is a mountainous country with a ridge of volcanoes running parallel to the Pacific coast. It has a tropical climate with little or no variation in temperature and a distinctive wet season. The Pacific slopes of the mountains are exceptionally well watered and fertile and it is here that most of the population are settled. Coffee growing on the lower slopes dominates the economy. A small strip on the coast produces sugar, cotton and bananas. Industry is mainly restricted to the processing of the agricultural products. Guatemala is politically a very unstable country and civil conflict has practically destroyed tourism.

Area : 108 889sq km (42 042sq mi)
Population : 9 000 000
Capital : Guatemala City
Other major city : Puerto
Barrios, Quezaltenango
Form of government :
Republic
Religion : RC
Currency : Quetzal

GUIANA (FRENCH)

Guiana is situated on the northeast coast of South America and is still an overseas department of France. It is bounded to the south and east by Brazil and to the west by Suriname. The climate is tropical with heavy rainfall. Guiana's economy relies almost completely on subsidies from France. It has little to export apart from shrimps and the small area of land which is cultivated produces rice, manioc and sugar cane. Recently the French have tried to develop the tourist industry and exploit the extensive reserves of hardwood in the jungle interior.

Area : 90 000sq km
(34 749sq mi)
Population : 73 800
Capital : Cayenne
Form of government :
French overseas department
Religion : RC
Currency : Franc

GUINEA

Guinea, formerly a French West African territory is located on the coast at the 'bulge' in Africa. It is a lush green beautiful country about the same size as the United Kingdom. It has a tropical climate with constant heat and a high rainfall near the coast. Guinea has great agricultural potential and many of the coastal swamps and forested plains have been cleared for the cultivation of rice, cassava, yams, maize and vegetables. Further inland on the plateaus of Futa Jalem dwarf cattle are raised and in the valleys bananas and pineapples are grown. Coffee and Kola nuts are important cash crops grown in the Guinea highlands in the southwest . Minerals such as bauxite, iron ore and diamonds are mined but development is hampered by lack of transport.

Area : 245 857sq km
(94 925sq mi)
Population : 6 710 000
Capital : Conakry
Other major city : Kankan,
Labé
Form of government :
Republic
Religion :Sunni Islam
Currency : Guinea franc

GUINEA BISSAU

Formerly a Portuguese territory Guinea Bissau is located south of Senegal on the Atlantic coast of West Africa. It is a country of stunning scenery and rises from a deeply indented and island fringed coastline to a low inland plateau. The adjacent Bijagos archipelago forms part of its territory. The climate is tropical with abundant rain from June to November but hot dry conditions for the rest of the year. Years of Portuguese rule and civil war have left Guinea Bissau impoverished and it is one of the poorest West African states. The country's main aim is to become self-sufficient in food and the main crops grown are groundnuts, sugar cane, plantains, coconuts and rice. Fishing is an important export industry.

Area : 36 125sq km
(13 948sq mi)
Population : 966 000
Capital : Bissau
Form of government :
Republic
Religion : Animist,
Sunni Islam
Currency : Peso

GUYANA

Guyana, the only English speaking country in South America, is situated on the northeast coast of the continent on the Atlantic Ocean. The country is intersected by many rivers and the coastal area comprises tidal marshes and mangrove swamps. It is on this coastal area that rice is grown and vast plantations produce sugar. The jungle in the southwest has potential for the production of minerals, hardwood and hydroelectric power, but 90% of the population live in the coastal area where the climate is moderated by sea breezes. The country is deeply divided politically and nothing has been done to improve productivity with the result that today the country is in an economic crisis.

Area : 214 969sq km (83 000sq mi)
Population : 990 000
Capital : Georgetown
Other major city : New Amsterdam
Form of government :
Cooperative republic
Religion : Hindu, Protestant, RC
Currency : Guyana dollar

HAITI

Haiti occupies the western third of the large island of Hispaniola in the Caribbean. It is a mountainous country, the highest point reaching 2680m at La Selle. The mountain ranges are separated by deep valleys and plains. The climate is tropical but semi-arid conditions can occur in the lee of the central mountains. Hurricanes and severe thunderstorms are a common occurrence. Only a third of the country is arable, yet agriculture is the chief occupation. Many farmers grow only enough to feed their own families and the export crops, coffee, sugar and sisal are grown on large estates. Severe soil erosion caused by extensive forest clearance has resulted in a decline in crop yields. Haiti is the poorest country in the Americas and has experienced many uprisings and attempted coups, the most recent being in January 1991.

Area : 27 750sq km
(10 714sq mi)
Population : 5 700 000
Capital : Port-au-Prince
Other major city : Les Cayes,
Jérémie, Gonaîves
Form of government :
Republic
Religion : RC, Voodoo
Currency : Gourde

HONDURAS

Honduras is a fan shaped country in Central America which spreads out into the Caribbean Sea of the Gulf of Honduras. Four-fifths of the country is covered in mountains which are indented with river valleys running towards the very short Pacific coast. There is little change in temperatures throughout the year and rainfall is heavy, especially on the Caribbean coast where temperatures are also higher than inland. The country is sparsely populated and although agricultural, only about 25% of the land is cultivated. Honduras was once the world's leading banana exporter and although its main export agriculture is more diverse. Grains, coffee and sugar are now important crops and these are grown mainly on the coastal plains of the Pacific and Caribbean. The forests are not effectively exploited and industry is small scale.

Area : 112 088sq km
(43 277sq mi)
Population : 4 440 000
Capital : Tegucigalpa
Form of government :
Republic
Religion : RC
Currency : Lempira

HONG KONG

The territory of Hong Kong is located in the South China Sea and consists of Hong Kong Island (once a barren rock), the peninsula of Kowloon and about 1000sq km of adjacent land known as the New Territories. Hong Kong is situated at the mouth of the Pearl River about 130Km southeast of Guangzhou (Canton). The climate is warm subtropical with cool dry winters and hot humid summers. Hong Kong has no natural resources, even its water comes from reservoirs across the Chinese border. Its main assets are its magnificent natural harbour and its position close to the main trading routes of the Pacific. Hong Kong's economy is based on free enterprise and trade, an industrious work force and an efficient and aggressive commercial system. Hong Kong's main industry is textiles and clothing which accounts for 38% of its domestic exports.

Area : 1 045sq km (403sq mi)
Population : 5 760 000
Form of government : Colony under British admin until 1997 when China will take over
Religion : Buddhist, Taoist, Christian
Currency : Hong Kong dollar

80

HUNGARY

Landlocked in the heartland of Europe, Hungary is dominated by the great plain to the east of the river Danube which runs north-southacross the country. In the west lies the largest lake in Central Europe, Lake Balaton. Winters are severe, but the summers are warm and although wet in the west, summer droughts often occur in the east. Hungary experienced a modest boom in its economy in the 1970s and 1980s. The government invested money in improving agriculture by mechanising farms, using fertilisers and bringing new land under cultivation. Yields of cereals for breadmaking and rice have since soared and large areas between the Danube and Tisza rivers are now used to grow vegetables. Industries have been carefully developed where adequate natural resources exist. New industries like electrical and electronic equipment are now being promoted and tourism is fast developing around Lake Balaton.

Area : 93 032sq km (35 920sq mi)
Population : 10 590 000
Capital : Budapest
Other major city : Debrecen, Miscolc, Szeged, Pécs
Form of government : Republic
Religion : RC, Calvanist, Lutheran
Currency : Forint

81

ICELAND

Iceland is a large island situated in an unstable part of the North Atlantic Ocean, just south of the Atlantic Circle. The island has over 100 volcanoes, at least one of which erupts every five years. One ninth of the country is covered with ice and snowfields and there are about seven hundred hot springs which are an important source of central heating. The climate is cool temperate but because of the effect of the North Atlantic Drift it is mild for its latitude. The southwest corner is the most densely populated area as the coast here is generally free from ice. Only 1% of the land is cultivated mostly for fodder and root crops to feed sheep and cattle. The island's economy is based on its sea fishing industry which accounts for 70% of exports. Wool sweaters and sheepskin coats are also exported.

Area : 103 000sq km
(39 768sq mi)
Population : 253 500
Capital : Reykjavík
Form of government :
Republic
Religion : Lutheran
Currency : Icelandic króna

INDIA

India is a vast country in South Asia which is dominated in the extreme north by the world's youngest and highest mountains, the Himalayas. At the foot of the Himalayas, a huge plain, drained by the Indus and Ganges rivers, is one of the most fertile areas in the world and the most densely populated part of India. Further south the ancient Deccan plateau extends to the southern tip of the country. India generally has four seasons, the cool, the hot, the rainy and the dry. Rainfall varies from 100mm in the northwest desert to 10 000mm in Assam. About 70% of the population depend on agriculture for their living and the lower slopes of the Himalayas represent one of the world's best tea growing areas. Rice, sugar cane and wheat are grown in the Ganges plain. An increase in the production of food is needed to support the rapidly growing population.

Area : 3 287 590sq km
(1 269 338sq mi)
Population : 843 930 000
Capital : New Delhi
Other major city : Calcutta,
Bombay, Delhi, Madras,
 Bangalore, Hyderabad
Form of government : Federal republic
Religion : Hindu, Sunni Islam, Christian
Currency : Rupee

INDONESIA

Indonesia is made up of 13 667 islands which are scattered across the Indian and Pacific Oceans in a huge crescent. It is the world's fifth largest country and its largest landmass is the province of Lalimantan which is part of the island of Borneo. Sumatra is the largest individual island. Java, however, is the dominant and most densely populated island. The climate is generally tropical monsoon and temperatures are high all year round. The country has one hundred volcanoes, and earthquakes are frequent in the southern islands. Overpopulation is a big problem especially in Java, where its fertile rust coloured soil is in danger of becoming exhausted. Rice, maize and cassava are the main crops grown. Indonesia has the largest reserves of tin in the world and is one of the world's leading rubber producers. Indonesia's resources are not as yet fully developed but there is great potential for economic development.

Area : 1 904 569sq km (735 354sq mi)
Population : 179 100 000
Capital : Jakarta
Other major city : Surabaya,
Badung, Medan, Semarang
Form of government : Republic
Religion : Sunni Islam, Christian, Hindu
Currency : Rupiah

IRAN

Across the Gulf from the Arabia peninsula is Iran, a country which stretches from the Caspian Sea to the Arabian Sea. It is a land dominated by mountains in the north and west, with a huge expanse of desert in its centre. The climate is mainly desert, although more temperate conditions are found on the shores of the Caspian Sea. In winter terrible dust storms sweep the deserts and almost no life can survive. Most of the population live in the north and west where Tehran is situated. The only good agricultural land is on the Caspian coastal plains and here rice is grown. About 5% of the population are nomadic herdsmen who wander in the mountains. Most of Iran's oil is in the southwest and other valuable minerals include coal, iron ore, copper and lead. Precious stones are found in the north east. The main exports are petrochemicals, carpets and rugs, textiles, raw cotton and leather goods.

Area : 1 648 000sq km
(636 293sq mi)
Population : 53 920 000
Capital : Tehran
Other major city : Esfahan,
Mashhad, Tabriz
Form of government :
Islamic Republic

IRAQ

Iraq is located in southwest Asia, wedged between the Gulf and Syria. It is almost landlocked except for its outlet to the Gulf at Shatt al Arab. Its two great rivers, the Tigres and the Euphrates, flow from the northwest into the Gulf at this point. The climate is arid with very hot summers and cold winters. The high mountains on the border with Turkey are snow covered for six months of the year, and desert in the southwest covers nearly half of the country. The only fertile land in Iraq is in the basins of the Tigres and Euphrates where wheat, barley, rice, tobacco and cotton are grown. The world's largest production of dates also comes from this area. Iraq profited from the great oil boom of the 1970s, but during the war with Iran oil terminals in the Gulf were destroyed and the trans-Syrian pipeline closed. Iraq is now wholly reliant on the pipeline from Kirkuk to the Mediterranean.

Area : 438 317sq km
(169 234sq mi)
Population : 17 060 000
Capital : Baghdad
Other major city : Al-Basrah,
Mosul
Form of government : Republic
Religion : Shia Islam, Sunni Islam
Currency : Iraqi dinar

86

IRELAND, REPUBLIC OF

The Republic of Ireland is one of Europe's most westerly islands, situated in the Atlantic Ocean and separated from Great Britain by the Irish Sea. It has an equable climate, with mild southwest winds which makes temperatures uniform over most of the country. The republic extends over four-fifths of the island of Ireland and the west and southwest is mountainous, with the highest peak reaching 1041m at Carauntoohil. The central plain is largely limestone covered in boulder clay which provides good farmland and pasture. Despite the fertile land the Republic of Ireland remains one of the poorest countries in western Europe. The rural population tend to migrate to the cities, mainly Dublin, which is the main industrial centre, centre of publishing and printing, and the focus of radio, television and communications. Lack of energy resources and remoteness from major markets has slowed industrial development.

Area : 70 284sq km (27 137sq mi)
Population : 3 540 000
Capital : Dublin
Other major city : Cork,
Limerick, Galway, Waterford
Form of government : Republic
Religion : RC
Currency : Irish pound

ISRAEL

Israel occupies a long narrow stretch of land in the southeast of the Mediterranean. Its eastern boundary is formed by the Great Rift Valley, through which the river Jordan flows to the Dead Sea. The south of the country is made up of a triangular wedge of the Neger Desert which ends at the Gulf of Aqaba. The climate in summer is hot and dry, in winter it is mild with some rain. The south of the country is arid and barren. Most of the population live on the coastal plain bordering the Mediterranean where Tel Aviv is the main commercial city. Israel's agriculture is based on collective settlements known as Kibbutz. The country is virtually self-sufficient in food stuffs and a major exporter of its produce. Jaffa oranges are famous throughout Europe. A wide range of products is processed or finished in the country and main exports are finished diamonds, textiles, fruit, vegetables, chemicals, machinery and fertilisers.

Area : 20 770sq km (8 019sq mi)
Population : 4 820 000
Capital : Jerusalem
Other major city : Tel Aviv,Haifa
Form of government : Republic
Religion : Judaism, Sunni Islam, Christian
Currency : Shekel

ITALY

Italy is a republic in southern Europe, which comprises a large peninsula and the two main islands of Sicily and Sardinia. The Alps form a natural boundary with its northern and western European neighbours and the Adriatic Sea to the east separates it from Yugoslavia. The Appenine Mountains form the backbone of Italy and extend the full length of the peninsula. Between the Alps and the Appenines lies the Po valley, a great fertile lowland. Sicily and Sardinia are largely mountainous. Much of Italy is geologically unstable and it has four active volcanoes, including Etna and Vesuvius. Italy enjoys warm dry summers and mild winters. The north is the main industrial centre and agriculture is well mechanised. In the south farms are small and traditional. Industries in the north include motor vehicles, textiles, clothing, leather goods, glass and ceramics. Tourism is an important source of foreign currency.

Area : 310 268sq km (116 320sq mi)
Population : 57 600 000
Capital : Rome
Other major city : Milan, Naples,
Turin, Genoa, Palermo
Form of government : Republic
Religion : RC
Currency : Lira

JAMAICA

The island of Jamaica lies in the Caribbean Sea about 150km south of Cuba. The centre of the island comprises a limestone plateau and this is surrounded by narrow coastal flatlands and palm fringed beaches. The highest mountains, the Blue Mountains, are in the east of the island. The climate is tropical with high temperatures at the coast, with slightly cooler and less humid conditions in the highlands. The island lies right in the middle of the hurricane zone. The traditional crops grown are sugar, bananas, peppers, ginger, cocoa and coffee, and new crops such as winter vegetables fruit and honey are being developed for export. Despite this the decline in the principal export products, bauxite and alumina, has resulted in near economic stagnation. Tourism is an important industry, as is the illegal trade in cannabis.

Area : 10 990sq km
(4 243sq mi)
Population : 2 400 000
Capital : Kingston
Other major city :
Montego Bay,
Spanish Town
Form of government : Constitutional monarchy
Religion : Anglican, other Protestant, RC
Currency : Jamaican dollar

JAPAN

Japan is located on the eastern margin of Asia and consists of four major islands, Honshu, Hokkaido, Kyushu and Shikoku, and many small islands. It is separated from the mainland of Asia by the Sea of Japan. The country is made up of six chains of steep serrated mountains, which contain about 60 active volcanoes. Earthquakes are frequent and widespread and often accompanied by giant waves (tsunami). Summers are warm and humid and winters mild, except on Hokkaido which is covered in snow in winter. Japan's agriculture is highly advanced with extensive use made of fertilisers and miniature machinery for the small fields. Fishing is important.. Japan is the second largest industrial economy in the world. It is very dependant on imported raw materials and its success is based on manufacturing industry which employs about one-third of the workforce.

Area : 377 801sq km
(145 869sq mi)
Population : 123 260 000
Capital : Tokyo
Other major city : Osaka,
Nagoya, Sapporo, Kobe, Kyoto
Form of government :
Constitutional monarchy
Religion : Shinto, Buddhist, Christian
Currency : Yen

JORDAN

Almost landlocked except for a short coastline on the Gulf of Aqaba, Jordan is bounded by Saudi Arabia, Syria, Iraq and Israel. Almost 80% of the country is desert and the rest comprises the East Bank Uplands and Jordan Valley. In general summers are hot and dry and winters cool and wet, with variations related to altitude. The east has a desert climate. Only one-fifth of the country is fertile enough to be farmed but the country is self-sufficient in potatoes, onions and poultry meat. The agricultural system is intensive and efficient. Amman is the main industrial centre of the country and the industries include phosphates, petroleum products, cement, iron and fertilisers. The rich Arab states such as Saudi Arabia give Jordan substantial economic aid.

Area : 97 740sq km
(37 737sq mi)
Population : 3 170 000
Capital : Amman
Other major city : Irbid, Zarga
Form of government :
Constitutional monarchy
Religion : Sunni Islam
Currency : Jordan dinar

KENYA

Located in east Africa, Kenya straddles the equator and extends from Lake Victoria in the southwest, to the Indian Ocean in the southeast. Highlands run north to south through central Kenya and are divided by the steep-sided Rift Valley. The coastal lowlands have a hot humid climate but in the highlands it is cooler and rainfall heavier. In the east it is very arid. The southwestern region is well watered with huge areas of fertile soil and this accounts for the bulk of the population and almost all its economic production. The main crops grown for domestic consumption are wheat and maize. Tea, coffee, sisal, sugar cane and cotton are grown for export. Oil refining at Mombasa is the country's largest single factory and other industry includes food processing and textiles. Tourism is an important source of foreign revenue.

Area : 580 367sq km
(224 080sq mi)
Population : 24 080 000
Capital : Nairobi
Other major cities : Mombasa, Kisumu
Form of government : Republic
Religions : RC, Protestant, other Christian, Animist
Currency : Kenya shilling

KIRIBATI

Kiribati comprises three groups of coral atolls and one isolated volcanic island spread over a large expanse of the central Pacific. The group includes Banaba Island, the Phoenix Islands and some of the Line Islands. The climate is maritime equatorial with a high rainfall. Most islanders are involved in subsistence agriculture. The principal tree is the coconut which grows well on all the islands. Palm and Breadfruit trees are also found. Soil is negligible and the only vegetable which can be grown is calladium. Tuna fishing is an important industry and Kiribati has granted licences to the USSR to fish its waters. Phosphate sources have now been exhausted and the country is heavily dependant on overseas aid.

Area : 726sq km (280sq mi)
Population : 66 250
Capital : Tarawa
Form of government :
Republic
Religions : RC, Protestant,
Currency : Australian dollar

KOREA, NORTH

North Korea occupies just over half of the Korean peninsula in east Asia. The Yala and Tumen rivers form its northern border with China and the USSR. Its southern border with South Korea is just north of the 38th parallel. It is a mountainous country, three-quarters of which is forested highland or scrubland. The climate is warm temperate, although winters can be cold in the north. Most rain falls during the summer. Nearly 90% of its arable land is farmed by cooperatives which employ over 40% of the labour force and rice is the main crop grown. North Korea is quite well endowed with fuel and minerals. Deposits of coal and hydroelectric power generate electricity, and substantial deposits of iron ore are found near Pyongyang and Musan. 60% of the labour force are employed in industry, the most important of which are metallurgical, building, cement and chemicals.

Area : 120 538sq km (46 540sq mi)
Population : 22 420 000
Capital : Pyongyang
Other major cities : Chongjin, Nampo
Form of government : Socialist Republic
Religions : Chondoist, Buddhist
Currency : North Korea won

KOREA, SOUTH

South Korea occupies the southern half of the Korean peninsula and stretches about 400km, from the Korea straight to the demilitarised zone bordering North Korea. It is predominantly mountainous with the highest ranges running north to south along the east coast. The west is lowland which is extremely densely populated. The extreme south has a humid warm temperate climate while further north it is more continental. Most rain falls in summer. Cultivated land represents only 23% of the country's total area and the main crop is rice. The country has few natural resources but has a flourishing manufacturing industry and is the world's leading supplier of ships and footwear. Other important industries are electronic equipment, electrical goods, steel, petrochemicals, motor vehicles and toys. Its people enjoy a reasonably high standard of living brought about by hard work and determination.

Area : 99 016sq km
(38 230sq mi)
Population : 42 800 000
Capital : Seoul
Other major cities : Pusan,
Taegu, Inchon
Form of government : Republic
Religions : Buddhist, Christian
Currency : South Korean Won

KUWAIT

Kuwait is a tiny Arab state on The Gulf, which comprises the city of Kuwait at the southern entrance of Kuwait Bay and a small undulating desert wedged between Iraq and Saudi Arabia. It has nine small offshore islands. It has a dry desert climate which is cool in winter but very hot and humid in summer. There is little agriculture due to lack of water and major crops produced are melons, tomatoes, onions and dates. Shrimp fishing is becoming an important industry. Large reserves of petroleum and natural gas are the mainstay of the economy. It has about 950 oil wells, however 600 were fired during the Iraqi occupation and are unlikely to resume production until 1992. Apart from oil, industry includes, boat building, food production, petrochemicals, gases and construction.

Area : 17 818sq km (6 880sq mi)
Population : 2 040 000
Capital : Kuwait
Form of government :
Constitutional monarchy
Religion : Sunni Islam,
Shia Islam
Currency : Kuwait dinar

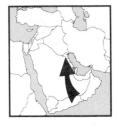

LAOS

Laos is a landlocked country in southeast Asia which is ruggedly mountainous, apart from the Mekong river plains along its border with Thailand. The Annam mountains, which reach 2 500m, form a natural border with Vietnam. It has a tropical monsoon climate with high temperatures throughout the year and heavy rains in summer. Laos is one of the poorest countries in the world and its development has been retarded by war, drought and floods. The principal crop is rice, grown on small peasant plots. There is some export of timber, coffee and electricity. All manufactured goods must be imported. The capital and largest city, Vientiane, is the country's main trade outlet via Thailand.

Area : 236 800sq km
(91 428sq mi)
Population : 4 050 000
Capital : Vientiane
Form of government :
People's republic
Religion : Buddhist
Currency : Kip

LATVIA

The newly formed republic of Latvia is located in northeast Europe on the Baltic Sea and is sandwiched between Estonia and Lithuania. Latvians traditionally lived by forestry, fishing and livestock rearing. The chief agricultural occupation are cattle and dairy farming and the main crops grown are oats, barley, rye, potatoes and flax. Latvia's population is now 70% urban and agriculture is no longer the mainstay of the economy. Cities such as Riga; the capital, Daugavpils, Ventspils and Liepaja now produce high quality textiles, machinery, electrical appliances, paper, chemicals, furniture and foodstuffs. Latvia has extensive deposits of peat which is used to manufacture briquettes. It also has deposits of gypsum and in the coastal areas amber is frequently found.

Area : 63 700sq km
(24 595sq mi)
Population : 2 681 000
Capital : Riga
Other major cities : Daugavpils,
Jurmala, Liepaja
Form of government : Republic
Religion : Lutheran
Currency : Ruble

LEBANON

Lebanon is a mountainous country in the eastern Mediterranean. A narrow coastal plain runs parallel to its 240km Mediterranean coast and gradually rises to the spectacular Lebanon Mountains, which are snow covered in winter. The Anti Lebanon mountains form the border with Syria and between the two ranges lies the Bekaa Valley. The climate is Mediterranean with short warm winters and long hot and rainless summers. Rainfall can be torrential in winter and snow falls on high ground. Lebanon is an agricultural country, the main regions of production being the Bekaa Valley and the Coastal plains. Main products include olives, grapes, citrus fruits, apples, cotton, tobacco and sugar beet. Industry is small scale and manufactures include, cement, fertilisers and jewellery. There are oil refineries at Tripoli and Sidon.

Area : 10 400sq km (4 015sq mi)
Population : 2 800 000
Capital : Beirut
Other important cities : Tripoli, Zahle
Form of government : Republic
Religions : Shia Islam, Sunni Islam, Christian
Currency : Lebanese pound

LESOTHO

Lesotho is a small landlocked kingdom entirely surrounded by the Republic of South Africa. Snow capped mountains and treeless uplands, cut by spectacular gorges, cover two-thirds of the country. The climate is pleasant with variable rainfall. Winters are generally dry with heavy frosts in lowland areas and frequent snow in the highlands. Due to the mountainous terrain, only one-eighth of the land can be cultivated and the main crop is maize. Yields are low because of soil erosion on the steep slopes and over-grazing by herds of sheep and cattle. Wool, mohair and diamonds are exported but most foreign exchange comes from money sent home by Lesotho workers in South Africa. Tourism is beginning to flourish, the main attraction to South Africans being the casinos in the capital Maseru, as gambling is prohibited in their own country.

Area : 30 355sq km
(11 720sq mi)
Population : 1 720 000
Capital : Maseur
Form of government :
Monarchy
Religions : RC, other Christian
Currency : Loti

LIBERIA

Liberia is located in West Africa and has a 560km coast stretching from Sierra Leone to Cote d'Ivoire. It is the only African country never to be ruled by a foreign power. It has a treacherous coast with rocky cliffs and lagoons enclosed by sand bars. Inland the land rises to a densely forested plateau dissected by deep, narrow valleys. Further inland still, there are beautiful waterfalls and the Nimba Mountains rise to over 1 700m. Agriculture employs three-quarters of the labour force and produces cassava and rice as subsistence crops and rubber, coffee and cocoa for export. The Nimba Mountains are rich in Iron Ore which accounts for 70% of export earnings. There is potential for tourism to develop. Forest and animal reserves are magnificent and the beaches and lagoons are beautiful but so far the facilities are very average.

Area : 111 369sq km
(43 000sq mi)
Population : 2 440 000
Capital : Monrovia
Form of government : Republic
Religion : Animist, Sunni
Islam, Christian
Currency : Liberian dollar

LIBYA

Libya is a large north African country which stretches from the south coast of the Mediterranean to, and in some parts beyond, the Tropic of Cancer. The Sahara Desert covers much of the country extending right to the Mediterranean coast at the Gulf of Sirte. The only green areas are the scrublands found in the northwest and the forested hills near Benghazi. The coastal area has mild wet winters and hot dry summers but the interior has had some of the highest recorded temperature of anywhere in the world. Only 14% of the people work on the land, the main agricultural region being in the northwest near Tripoli. Many sheep, goats and cattle are reared and there is an export trade in skins, hides and hairs. Libya is one of the world's largest producers of oil and natural gas. Other industries include food processing, textiles, cement and handicrafts.

Area : 1 759 540sq km (679 358sq mi)
Population : 4 000 000
Capital : Tripoli
Other major cities : Benghazi, Misurata
Form of government : Socialist state
Religion : Sunni Islam
Currency : Libyan dinar

LIECHTENSTEIN

The principality of Liechtenstein is a tiny central European state situated on the east bank of the river Rhine and is bounded by Austria to the east and Switzerland to the west. In the east of the principality the Alps rise to 2599m at Grauspitze. The climate is mild alpine. Once an agricultural country, Liechtenstein has rapidly moved into industry in the last thirty years. It has a great variety of light industries such as textiles, high quality metal goods, precision instruments, pharmaceuticals and ceramics. It is a popular location for foreign companies to have their headquarters in order that they can benefit from the country's lenient tax laws. Tourism is also big business, beautiful scenery and good skiing being the main attractions.

Area : 160sq km (62sq mi)
Population : 28 181
Capital : Vaduz
Form of government :
Constitutional monarchy
Religion : RC
Currency : Swiss franc

LITHUANIA

Lithuania lies to the northwest of the USSR and is bounded to the north by Latvia and west by Poland. It is the largest of the three former soviet Baltic Republics. Before 1940 Lithuania was a mainly agricultural country but has since been considerably industrialised. Most of the land is lowland covered by forest and swamp and the main products are rye, barley, sugar beet, flax, meat, milk and potatoes. Industry includes heavy engineering, shipbuilding and building materials. Oil production has started from a small field at Kretinga. Amber is found along the Baltic coast and used by Lithuanian craftsmen for making jewellery.

Area : 65 200sq km
(25 174sq mi)
Population : 3 690 000
Capital : Vilnius
Other major cities : Kaunas,
Klaipeda, Siauliai
Form of government :
Republic
Religion : RC
Currency : Ruble

LUXEMBOURG

The Grand Duchy of Luxembourg is a small independent country bounded by Belgium on the west, France on the south and Germany on the east. In the north of the Duchy a wooded plateau, the Oesling, rises to 550m and in the south a lowland area of valleys and ridges is known as the Gutland. Northern winters are cold and raw with snow covering the ground for almost a month, but in the south winters are mild and summers cool. In the south the land is fertile and crops grown include maize, roots, tubers and potatoes. Dairy farming is also important. It is in the south, also, that beds of iron ore are found and these form the basis of the country's iron and steel industry. In the east Luxembourg is bordered by the Moselle river in whose valley wines are produced.

Area : 2 586sq km (998sq mi)
Population : 378 400
Capital : Luxembourg
Form of government :
Constitutional monarchy
Religion : RC
Currency : Luxembourg franc

MADAGASCAR

Situated off the southeast coast of Africa, Madagascar is separated from the mainland by the Mozambique Channel. Madagascar is the fourth largest island in the world and the centre of it is made up of high savanna-covered plateau. In the east, forested mountains fall steeply to the coast and in the southwest, the land falls gradually through dry grassland and scrub. The staple food crop is rice and 80% of the population grow enough to feed themselves. Cassava is also grown but some 58% of the land is pasture and there are more cattle than people. The main export earners are coffee, vanilla, cloves and sugar. There is some mining for chromite and an oil refinery at Toamasina on the east coast.

Area 587 041sq km
(226 657sq mi)
Population : 11 440 000
Capital : Antananavivo
Other major cities : Toamasina,
Mahajanga, Fianarantsoa
Form of government : Republic
Religions : Animist, RC,
Protestant
Currency : Malagasy franc

MALAWI

Malawi lies along the southern and wester shores of the third largest lake in Africa, Lake Nyasa. To the south of the lake the Shive river flows through a valley, overlooked by wooded, towering mountains. The tropical climate has a dry season from May to October and a wet season for the remaining months. Agriculture is the predominant occupation and many Malawians live on their own crops. Plantation farming is used for export crops. Tea is grown on the terraced hillsides in the south and tobacco on the central plateau. Malawi has bauxite and coal deposits but due to the inaccessibility of their locations, mining is limited. Hydroelectricity is now being used for the manufacturing industry but imports of manufactured goods remain high.

Area : 118 484sq km
(45 747sq mi)
Population : 7 980 000
Capital : Lilongwe
Other major cities : Blantyre,
Mzuzu, Zomba
form of government : Republic
Religions : Animist, RC,
Presbyterian
Currency : Kwacha

MALAYSIA

The Federation of Malaysia lies in the South China Sea in southeast Asia, and comprises Peninsular Malaysia on the Malay peninsula and the states of Sabah and Sarowak on the island of Borneo. Malaysia is affected by the monsoon climate. The northeast monsoon brings rain to the east coast of Peninsular Malaysia in winter, and the southwest monsoon brings rain to the west coast in summer. Throughout the country the climate is generally tropical and temperatures are uniformly hot throughout the year. Peninsular Malaysia has always had thriving rubber-growing and tin dredging industries and now oil palm growing is also important on the east coast. Sabah and Sarawak have grown rich by exploiting their natural resources, the forests. There is also some offshore oil and around the capital, Kuala Lumpur, new industries such as electronics are expanding.

Area : 329 749sq km
(127 316sq mi)
Population : 17 810 000
Capital : Kuala Lumpur
Other major cities : Ipoh,
Georgetown, Johor Baharu
Form of government : Federal
constitutional monarchy
Religion : Sunni Islam
Currency : Malaysian ringgit

MALDIVES

The Republic of Maldives lies 640km southwest of Sri Lanka in the Indian Ocean and comprises 1200 low lying coral islands grouped into 12 atolls. Only about 202 of the islands are inhabited and the highest point is only 1.5m above sea level. The climate is hot and humid and affected by monsoons between May and August. The islands are covered with coconut palms and some millet, cassava yams and tropical fruit are grown. Rice however, the staple diet of its islanders, has to be imported. Fishing is an important occupation and the chief export is now canned or frozen tuna, most of which goes to Japan. Tourism is now developing fast and has taken over fishing as the major foreign currency earner.

Area 298sq km (115sq mi)
Population : 214 139
Capital : Male
form of government : Republic
Religion : Sunni Islam
Currency : Rufiyaa

MALI

Mali is a landlocked state in west Africa. The country mainly comprises vast and monotonous plains and plateaux. It rises to 1155m in the Adrar des Iforas range in the north east. The Sahara in the north of the country is encroaching southwards and the country is one of the poorest in the world. In the south there is some rain and plains are covered by grassy savanna and a few scattered trees. The river Niger runs through the south of the country and small steamboats use it for shipping between Koulikoro and Gao. Only one-fifth of the land can be cultivated. Rice, cassava and millet are grown for domestic consumption and cotton for export. Droughts in the early 1970s resulted in thousands of cattle dying, crop failure and famine and disease killing many of the population. Iron ore and bauxite has been discovered but as yet have not been mined.

Area : 1 240 192sq km
(478 838sq mi)
Population : 9 090 000
Capital : Bamako
Other major cities : Segou, Mopti
form of government : Republic
Religions : Sunni Islam, Animist
Currency : Franc CFA

MALTA

Malta, a small republic in the middle of the Mediterranean, lies just south of the islands of Sicily. It comprises three islands, Malta, Gozo and Comino, which are made up of low limestone plateaux with little surface water. The climate is Mediterranean with hot, dry sunny summers and little rain. Winters are cooler and wetter. Malta is virtually self sufficient in agricultural products and exports potatoes, vegetables, wine and cut flowers. The British military base on Malta was once the mainstay of the economy but after the British withdrew in the late 1970s, the naval dockyard was converted for commercial shipbuilding and repairs, which is now one of the leading industries. Tourism has also boomed and the island has become popular for retirement in the sunshine with low taxes.

Area : 316sq km (122sq mi)
Population : 354 900
Capital : Valletta
Form of government : Republic
Religion : RC
Currency : Maltese pound

MAURITANIA

Mauritania, a country nearly twice the size of France, is located on the west coast of Africa. About 47% of the country is desert, the Sahara covering much of the north. The only settlements found in this area are around oases, where a little millet, dates and vegetables can be grown. The main agricultural regions are in the Senegal river valley in the south. The rest of the country is made up of the drought stricken sahel grasslands. The majority of the people are traditionally nomadic herdsmen but the severe droughts since the 1970s have killed about 70% of the nations animals and the population have settled along the Senegal river. As a result, vast shanty towns have sprung up around all the towns. Deposits of iron ore and copper provide the country's main exports and development of these and the fishing industry on the coast is the only hope for a brighter future.

Area : 1 025 520sq km
(395 953sq mi)
Population : 1 970 000
Capital : Nouakchott
Form of government :
Republic
Religion : Sunni Islam
Currency : Ouguiya

MAURITIUS

Mauritius is a beautiful island with tropical beaches which lies about 20° south in the Indian Ocean, 800km east of Madagascar. The islands of Rodrigues and Agalepa are also part of Mauritius. Mauritius is a volcanic island with many craters surrounded by lava flows. The central plateau rise to over 800m, then drops sharply to the south and west coasts. The climate is hot and humid and southwesterly winds bring heavy rain in the uplands. The island has well-watered fertile soil which is ideal for sugar plantations, which cover 45% of the island. Although the export of sugar still dominates the economy, diversification is being encouraged. The clothing and electronic equipment industries are becoming increasingly important and tourism is now the third largest source of foreign exchange.

Area : 2 040sq km (788sq mi)
Population : 1 081 669
Capital : Port Louis
Form of government :
Constitutional monarchy
Religions : Hindu, RC, Sunni
Islam
Currency : Mauritius rupee

MEXICO

Mexico, the most southerly country in North America, has its longest border with the USA to the north, a long coast on the Pacific Ocean and a smaller coast in the west of the gulf of Mexico. It is a land of volcanic mountain ranges and high plateaux. The highest peak is Citlaltepetl, which is permanently snow capped. Coastal lowlands are found in the west and east. Its wide range of latitude and relief, produce a variety of climates. In the north there are arid and semi arid conditions while in the south there is a humid tropical climate. 30% of the labour force are involved in agriculture growing maize, wheat, kidney beans and rice for subsistence and coffee, cotton, fruit and vegetables for export. Mexico is the world's largest producer of silver and has large reserves of oil and natural gas. Developing industries are petrochemicals, textiles, motor vehicles and food processing.

Area : 1 958 201sq km (756 061sq mi)
Population : 81 140 000
Capital : Mexico City
Other major cities : Guadalajara, Monterrey, Puebla de Zaragoza
Form of government : Federal republic
Religion : RC
Currency : Mexican peso

MONACO

Monaco is a tiny principality on the Mediterranean surrounded landwards by the Alpes Maritimes department of France. It comprises a rocky peninsula and a narrow stretch of coast. It has mild moist winters and hot dry summers. The old town of Monaco-Ville is situated on a rocky promontory and houses the royal palace and the cathedral. Monte Carlo has its world famous casino and La Condamine has thriving businesses, shops, banks and attractive residential areas. Fontvieille is an area reclaimed from the sea where now marinas and light industry are located. Light industry includes chemicals, plastics, electronics, engineering and paper but it is tourism that is the main revenue earner.

Area : 195 hectares (48 acres)
Population : 29 876
Capital : Monaco-Ville
Form of government :
Constitutional monarchy
Religion : RC
Currency : Franc

MONGOLIA

Mongolia is a landlocked country in northeast Asia which is bounded to the north by the USSR and by China to the south, west and east. Most of Mongolia is mountainous and over 1500m above sea level. In the northwest are the Hangayn Mountains and the Altai rising to 4362m. In the south there are grass covered steppes and desert wastes of the Gobi. The climate is very extreme and dry. For six months the temperatures are below freezing and the summers are mild. Mongolia has had a traditional nomadic pastoral economy for centuries and cereals including fodder crops are grown on a large scale on state farms. Industry is small scale and dominated by food processing. The mining industry has been developed at Darhan and Erdenet with aid from the USSR and copper accounts for 40% of the country's exports.

Area : 1 566 500sq km
(604 826sq mi)
Population : 2 095 000
Capital : Ulan Bator
Other major cities : Darhan, Erdenet
Form of government : Republic
Religion : Previously Buddhist but religion is now suppressed
Currency : Tugrik

MOROCCO

Morocco, in northwest Africa, is strategically placed at the western entrance to the Mediterranean Sea. It is a land of great contrasts with high rugged mountains, the arid Sahara and the green Atlantic and Mediterranean coasts. The country is split from southwest to northeast by the Atlas mountains. The north has a pleasant Mediterranean climate with hot dry summers and mild moist winters. Farther south winters are warmer and summers even hotter. Snow often falls in winter on the Atlas mountains. Morocco is mainly a farming country, wheat, barley and maize are the main food crops and it is one of the world's chief exporters of citrus fruit. Morocco's main wealth comes from phosphates, reserves of which are the largest in the world. The economy is very mixed. Morocco is self sufficient in textiles, it has car assembly plants, scrap and cement factories and a large sea fishing industry. Tourism is a major source of revenue.

Area : 446 550sq km (172 413sq mi)
Population : 24 500 000
Capital : Rabat
other major cities : Casablanca,
Fez, Marrakesh
Form of government :
Constitutional monarchy
Religion : Sunni Islam
Currency : Dirham

MOZAMBIQUE

Mozambique is a republic located in southeast Africa. A costal plain covers most of the southern and central territory, giving way to the western highlands and north to a plateau including the Myasa Highlands. The Zambezi river separates the high plateaux in the north from the lowlands in the south. The country has a humid tropical climate with highest temperatures and rainfall in the north. Normally conditions are reasonably good for agriculture but a drought in the early 1980s, followed a few years later by severe flooding, resulted in famine and more than 100 000 deaths. A lot of industry was abandoned when the Portuguese left the country and, due to lack of expertise, was not taken over by the local people. There is little incentive to produce surplus produce for cash and food rationing has now been introduced. This also has led to a black market which now accounts for a sizable part of the economy.

Area : 801 590sq km (309 494sq mi)
Population : 14 900 000
Capital : Maputo
Other major cities : Beira, Nampula
Form of government : Republic
Religions : Animist, RC, Sunni Islam
Currency : Metical

NAMIBIA

Namibia is situated on the Atlantic coast of southwest Africa. There are three main regions in the country. Running down the entire Atlantic coastline is the Namib Desert, east of which is the Central Plateau of mountains, rugged out crops, sandy valleys and poor grasslands. East again and north is the Kalahari Desert. Namibia has a poor rainfall, the highest falling at Windhoek, the capital. Even here it only amounts to 200-250mm per year. It is essentially a stock rearing country with sheep and goats raised in the south and cattle in the central and northern areas. Diamonds are mined just north of the river Orange and the largest open groove Uranium mine in the world is located near Swakopmund. One of Africa's richest fishing grounds lies off the coast of Namibia and mackerel, tuna and pilchards are an important export.

Area : 824 292sq km
(318 259sq mi)
Population : 1 290 000
Capital : Windhoek
Form of government : Republic
Religions : Lutheran, RC, other
Christian
Currency : Rand

NAURU

The world's smallest republic is the island of Nauru. It is situated just 40km south of the equator and is halfway between Australia and Hawaii. It is an oval shaped coral island only 20km in diameter and is surrounded by a reef. The centre of the island comprises a plateau which rises to 60m above sea level. The climate is tropical with a high and irregular rainfall. The country is rich, due entirely to the rich deposits of high quality phosphate rock in the central plateau. This is sold for fertiliser to Australia, New Zealand, Japan and South Korea. Phosphate deposits are likely to be exhausted by 1995 but the government is investing overseas.

Area : 21sq km (8sq mi)
Population : 8 100
Capital : Yaren
form of government :
Republic
Religions : Protestant, RC
Currency : Australian dollar

NEPAL

Nepal is a long narrow rectangular country, landlocked between China and India on the flanks of the eastern Himalayas. Its northern border runs along the mountain tops. In this border area is Everest, 8848m, the highest mountain in the world. The climate is subtropical in the south and all regions are affected by the monsoon. Nepal is one of the world's poorest and least developed countries with most of the population trying to survive as peasant farmers. It has no significant minerals, however with Indian and Chinese aid roads have been built from the north and south to Kathmandu. The construction of hydroelectric power schemes is now underway.

Area : 140 797sq km
(54 362sq mi)
Population : 18 000 000
Capital : Kathmandu
Form of government :
Constitutional monarchy
Religion : Hindu, Buddhist
Currency : Nepalese rupee

THE NETHERLANDS

Situated in northwest Europe, the Netherlands is bounded to the north and west by the North Sea. Over one-quarter of the Netherlands is below sea level and the Dutch have tackled some huge reclamation schemes to add some land area to the country. One such scheme is the Ijsselmeer, where four large areas reclaimed have added an extra 1650sq km for cultivation and an overspill town for Amsterdam. The Netherlands has mild winters and cool summers. Agriculture and horticulture are highly mechanised and the most notable feature is the sea of glass under which salad vegetables, fruit and flowers are grown. Manufacturing industries include chemicals, machinery, petroleum, refining, metallurgy and electrical engineering. The main port of the Netherlands, Rotterdam, is the largest in the world.

Area : 40 844sq km (15 770sq mi)
Population : 14 890 000
Capital : Amsterdam
Seat of government : The Hague
Other major cities : Rotterdam,
Utrecht, Eindhoven
Form of government :
Constitutional monarch
Religions :RC, Dutch reformed, Calvinist

123

NEW ZEALAND

New Zealand lies southeast of Australia in the South Pacific. It comprises two large islands, North Island and South Island, Stewart Island and the Chatham Islands. New Zealand enjoys very mild winters with regular rainfall and no extremes of heat or cold. North Island is hilly with isolated mountains and active volcanoes. On South Island the Southern Alps run north to south and the highest point is Mount Cook (3764m). The Canterbury Plains lie to the east of the mountains. Two-thirds of New Zealand is suitable for agriculture and grazing, meat, wool and dairy goods being the main products. Forestry supports the pulp and paper industry and considerable hydroelectric power potential produces cheap electricity for the manufacturing industry which now accounts for 30% of New Zealand's exports.

Area : 270 986sq km
(104 629sq mi)
Population : 3 390 000
Capital : Wellington
Other major cities : Auckland,
Christchurch, Dunedin,
Hamilton

Form of government : Constitutional monarchy
Religions : Anglican, RC, Presbyterian
Currency : New Zealand dollar

Nicaragua lies between the Pacific Ocean and the Caribbean Sea, on the isthmus of Central America, and is sandwiched between Honduras to the north and Costa Rica to the south. The east coast contains forested lowland and is the wettest part of the island. Behind this is a range of volcanic mountains and the west coast is a belt of savanna lowland running parallel to the Pacific coast. The western region, which contains the two huge lakes, Nicaragua and Managua, is where most of the population live. The whole country is subject to devastating earthquakes. Nicaragua is primarily an agricultural country and 65% of the labour force work on the land and the main export crops are coffee, cotton and sugar cane. All local industry is agriculture related.

Area : 130 000sq km
(50 193sq mi)
Population : 3 750 000
Capital : Managua
Form of government :
Republic
Religion : RC
Currency : Córdoba

NIGER

Niger is a landlocked republic in west Africa, lying just south of the Tropic of Cancer. Over half of the country is covered by the encroaching Sahara Desert, in the north and the south lies in the drought stricken Sahel. In the extreme southwest corner, the river Niger flows through the country and in the extreme southeast, lies Lake Chad but the rest of the country is extremely short of water. The people in the southwest fish and farm their own food, growing rice and vegetables on land flooded by the river. Farther from the river, crops have failed year after year as a result of successive droughts since 1968. Even in the north, where the population are traditionally herdsmen, drought has wiped out whole clans of tribesmen. Uranium mined in the Air mountains is Niger's main export.

Area : 1 267 000sq km
(489 189sq mi)
Population : 7 450 000
Capital : Niamey
Form of government :
Republic
Religion : Sunni Islam
Currency : Franc CFA

126

NIGERIA

Nigeria is a large and populous country in west Africa and from the Gulf of Guinea, it extends north to the border with Niger. It has a variable landscape, from the swampy coastal areas and tropical forest belts of the interior, to the mountains and savanna of the north. The two main rivers are the Niger and the Benue and just north of their confluence lies the Jos Plateau. The climate is hot and humid and rainfall, heavy at the coast, gradually decreases inland. The dry far north is affected by the Harmattan, a hot dry wind blowing from the Sahara. The main agricultural products are cocoa, rubber, groundnuts and cotton. However only cocoa is of any significance for export. The country depends on revenue from petroleum exports but fluctuations in the world oil market have left Nigeria with economic problems.

Area 923 768sq km (356 667sq mi)
Population : 118 700 000
Capital : Lagos (New federal
Capital under construction at Abiya)
Other major cities : Ibadan,
Ogbornsho, Kano
Form of government : Federal
republic
Religions : Sunni Islam, Christian
Currency : Naira

NORWAY

Norway occupies the western half of the Scandinavian peninsula in northern Europe, and is surrounded to the north, west and south by water. It shares most of its eastern border with Sweden. It is a country of spectacular scenery of fjords, cliffs, rugged uplands and forested valleys. Two-thirds of the country is over 600m and it has some of the deepest fjords in the world. The climate is temperate as a result of the warming effect of the Gulf Stream. Summers are mild and although the winters are long and cold, the waters off the west coast remain ice-free. Agriculture is chiefly concerned with dairying and fodder crops. Fishing is an important industry and the large reserves of forest provide timber for export. Industry is now dominated by the petrochemicals based on the reserves of Norwegian oil in the North Sea.

Area : 323 895sq km
(125 056sq mi)
Population : 4 200 000
Capital : Oslo
Other major cities : Bergen,
Trondheim, Stavanger
Form of government :
Constitutional monarchy
Religion : Lutheran
Currency : Norwegian krone

128

OMAN

Situated in the southeast of the Arabian peninsula, Oman is a small country in two parts. It comprises a small mountainous area, overlooking the straits of Hormuz, which controls the entrance to The Gulf, and the main port of the country, consisting of barren hills rising sharply behind a narrow coastal plain. Inland the hills extend into the unexplored 'Empty Quarter' in Saudi Arabia. Oman has a desert climate with exceptionally hot and humid conditions from April to October. Only 0.1% of country is cultivated, the main produce being dates. The economy is almost entirely dependent on oil which provides 90% of its exports. Oman has some deposits of copper and there is a smelter at Sohar.

Area : 212 457sq km
(82 030sq mi)
Population : 2 000 000
Capital : Muscat
Form of government :
Monarchy (sultanate)
Religion : Ibadi Islam,
Sunni Islam
Currency : Rial Omani

PAKISTAN

Pakistan lies just north of the Tropic of Cancer and has as its southern border the Arabian Sea. The valley of the Indus river splits the country into a highland region in the west, and a lowland region in the east. In the north are some of the world's highest mountains. The peak K2 (8611m) lies in Kashmir, a territory to which India also lays claim. A weak form of tropical monsoon climate occurs over most of the country and conditions in the north and west are arid. Temperatures are high everywhere in summer but winters are cold in the mountains. Most agriculture is subsistence, with wheat and rice as the main crops. Cotton is the main cash crop, however the cultivated area is restricted due to waterlogging and saline soils. Pakistan's wide range of mineral resources have not been extensively developed and industry concentrates on food processing, textiles and consumer goods.

Area : 796 095sq km (307 372sq mi)
Population : 105 400 000
Capital : Islamabad
Other major cities : Karachi, Lahore, Faisalabad, Hyderabad
Form of government : Federal Islamic republic
Religion : Sunni Islam, Shia Islam
Currency : Pakistan rupee

PANAMA

Panama is located at the narrowest point in Central America. Only 58km separates the Caribbean Sea from the Pacific Ocean at Panama, the Panama Canal which divides the country is the main routeway from the Caribbean and Atlantic to the Pacific. The climate is tropical with high temperatures throughout the year and only a short dry season from January to April. The country is heavily forested and very little is cultivated. Rice is the staple food. The economy is heavily dependent on the Canal and income from it is a major foreign currency earner. The country has great timber resources, and mahogany from these is an important export. Other exports are shrimps and bananas.

Area : 77 082sq km
(29 761sq mi)
Population : 2 320 000
Capital : Panama City
Other major cities :
San Miguelito, Colon
Form of government :
Republic
Religion : RC
Currency : Balboa

PAPUA NEW GUINEA

Papua New Guinea in the southwest Pacific, comprises the eastern half of the island of New Guinea, together with hundreds of islands of which New Britain, Bougainville and New Ireland are the largest. The country has a mountainous interior surrounded by broad swampy plains. The climate is tropical with high temperatures and heavy rainfall. Subsistence farming is the main economic activity although some coffee, cocoa and coconuts are grown for cash. Timber is cut for export and fishing and fish processing industries are developing. Minerals such as copper, gold, silver and oil form the mainstay of the economy. The country still receives valuable aid from Australia, who governed it before independence.

Area : 462 840sq km
(178 703sq mi)
Population : 3 800 000
Capital : Port Moresby
Form of government :
Constitutional monarchy
Religion : Protestant, RC
Currency : Kina

PARAGUAY

Paraguay, located in central South America, is a country without a coastline and is bordered by Bolivia, Brazil and Argentina. The climate is tropical with abundant rain and a short dry season. The river Paraguay splits the country into the Chaco, a flat semi arid plain on the west, and a partly forested undulating plateau on the east. Almost 95% of the population live east of the river, where crops grown on the fertile plains include cassava, sugar cane, maize, cotton and soya beans. Immediately west of the river, on the low Chaco, are huge cattle ranches which provide meat for export. The world's largest hydro-electric dam has been built at Itaipu and cheap power from this has stimulated industry. Industry includes food processing, vegetable oil refining, textiles and cement.

Area : 406 752sq km
(157 047sq mi)
Population : 4 160 000
Capital : Ascension
Other major city : Guidad
Alfredo Stroessner
Form of government : Republic
Religion : RC
Currency : Guarani

PERU

Peru is located just south of the equator, on the Pacific coast of South America. The country has three distinct regions from west to east, the coast, the high sierra of the Andes and the tropical jungle. The climate on the narrow coastal belt is mainly desert, while the Andes are wet, and east of the mountains is equatorial with tropical forests. Most large scale agriculture is in the oases and fertile, irrigated river valleys that cut across the coastal desert. Sugar and cotton are the main exports. Sheep, llamas, vicunas and alpacas are kept for wool. The fishing industry was once the largest in the world but recently the shoals have become depleted. Peru's main source of wealth is oil but new discoveries are needed, as present reserves are near exhaustion. In general, the economy has recently been damaged due to the declining value of exports, natural disasters and guerilla warfare.

Area : 1 285 216sq km (496 235sq mi)
Population : 22 330 000
Capital : Lima
Other major cities : Callao,
Arequipa, Trujillo, Cuzco
Form of government : Republic
Religion : RC
Currency : Sol

THE PHILIPPINES

The Philippines comprise a group of islands, in the western Pacific, which are scattered over a great area. There are four main groups, Luzon and Mindoro to the north, the Visayan Islands in the centre, Mindanao and the Sula archipelago in the south and Palawan in the southwest. Most of the island group is mountainous and earthquakes are common. The climate is humid with high temperatures and high rainfall. Typhoons are frequent. Rice and maize are the main subsistence crops and coconuts, sugar cane, pineapples and bananas are grown for export. Copper is a major export and there are deposits of gold, nickel and petroleum. Major industries include textiles, food processing chemicals and electrical engineering.

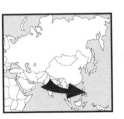

Area : 300 000sq km
(115 830sq mi)
Population : 60 500 000
Capital : Manilla
Other major cities :
Quezon City, Davae, Cebu
Form of government : Republic
Religions : RC, Aglipayan,
 Sunni Islam
Currency : Philippine peso

POLAND

Situated on the North European Plain, Poland borders
Germany to the west, Czechoslovakia to the south and
USSR to the east. Poland consists mainly of lowlands
and the climate is continental, marked by long severe
winters and short warm summers. Over one-quarter of
the labour force is involved in agriculture which is
predominantly small scale. The main crops are potatoes,
wheat, barley, sugar beet and fodder crops. The
industrial sector of the economy is large scale. Poland
has large deposits of coal and reserves of natural gas,
copper and silver. Vast forests stretching inland from
the coast supply the paper and furniture industries.
Other industries include food processing, engineering
and chemicals.

Area : 312 677sq km
(120 725sq mi)
Population : 37 930 000
Capital : Warsaw
Other major cities : Lódz,
Kraków, Wroclow, Gdansk
Form of government : Republic
Religion : RC
Currency : Zloty

PORTUGAL

Portugal, in the southwest corner of Europe, makes up about 15% of the Iberian peninsula. The most mountainous areas of Portugal lie to the north of the river Tagus. In the northeast are the steep sided mountains of Tras-os-Montes and south of this is the Douro valley, which runs from the Spanish border to Oporto, on the Atlantic coast. South of the Tagus river is the Alentajo, with its wheat fields and cork plantations, this continues to the hinterland of the Algarve with its beautiful groves of almond, fig and olive trees. Agriculture employs one-quarter of the labour force and crops include wheat and maize, as well as grapes and tomatoes. Manufacturing industry includes textiles and clothing for export, and footwear, food processing and cork products. Tourism is the main foreign currency earner.

Area : 92 389sq km (35 671sq mi)
Population : 10 300 000
Capital : Lisbon
Other major cities : Oporto,
Setúbal, Goimbra, Braga
Form of government : Republic
Religion : RC
Currency : Escudo

PUERTO RICO

Puerto Rico is the most easterly of the Greater Antilles and lies in the Caribbean between the Dominican Republic and the US Virgin Islands. It is a self-governing commonwealth in association with the USA and includes the main island, Puerto Rico, the two small islands of Vieques and Culebra and a fringe of smaller uninhabited islands. The climate is tropical, modified slightly by cooling sea breezes. The main mountains on Puerto Rico are the Gar Cordillera Central, which reach 1338m at the peak of Cerro de Punta. Dairy farming is the most important agricultural activity but the whole agricultural sector has been overtaken by industry in recent years. Tax relief and cheap labour encourages American businesses to be based in Puerto Rico. Products include textiles, clothing, electrical and electronic goods, plastics and chemicals. Tourism is another developing industry.

Area : 8 897sq km (3 435sq mi)
Population : 3 196 520
Capital : San Juan
Form of government :
Self governing
commonwealth(USA)
Relgion : RC,Protestant
Currency : US dollar

138

QATAR

Qatar is a little emirate which lies halfway along the coast of The Gulf. It consists of a low barren peninsula and a few small islands. The climate is hot and uncomfortably humid in summer and the winters are mild with rain in the north. Most fresh water comes from natural springs and wells or from desalination plants. The herding of sheep, goats and some cattle is carried out and the country is famous for its high quality camels. The discovery and exploitation of oil has resulted in a high standard of living for the people of Qatar. The Dukhan oil field has an expected life of forty years and the reserves of natural gas are enormous. In order to diversify the economy, new industries such as iron and steel, cement, fertilisers, and petrochemical plants have been developed.

Area : 11 000sq km
(4 247sq mi)
Population : 371 863
Capital : Doha
form of government :
Monarchy
Religions : Wahhabi
Sunni Islam
Currency : Qatari riyal

ROMANIA

Apart from a small extension towards the Black Sea, Romania is almost a circular country. It is located in southeast Europe and bordered by the USSR, Hungary, Yugoslavia and Bulgaria. The Carpathian Mountains run through the north, east and centre of Romania and these are enclosed by a ring of rich agricultural plains which are flat in the south and west but hilly in the east. The core of Romania is Transylvania within the Carpathian arc. Romania has cold snowy winters and hot summers. Agriculture in Romania has been neglected in favour of industry but major crops include maize, sugar beet, wheat, potatoes and grapes for wine. There are now severe food shortages. Industry is state owned and includes mining, metallurgy, mechanical engineering and chemicals. Forests support timber and furniture making industries in the Carpathians.

Area : 237 500sq km
(91 699sq mi)
Population 23 000 000
Capital : Bucharest
Other major cities : Brasov,
Constanta, Timisoara
Form of government : Republic
Religions : Romanian Orthodox, RC
Currency : Leu

RWANDA

Rwanda is a small republic in the heart of central Africa which lies just 2° south of the equator. It is a mountainous country with a central spine of highlands from which streams flow west to the Zaire river and east to the Nile. Active volcanoes are found in the north where the land rises to about 4500m. The climate is highland tropical with temperatures decreasing with altitude. The soils are not fertile and subsistence agriculture dominates the economy. Staple food crops are sweet potatoes, cassava, dry beans, sorghum and potatoes. The main cash crops are coffee, tea and pyrethrum. There are major reserves of natural gas under Lake Kivu in the west, but these are largely unexploited.

Area : 26 338sq km
(10 169sq mi)
Population : 6 710 000
Capital : Kigali
Form of government :
Republic
Religions : RC, Animist
Currency : Rwanda franc

ST. CHRISTOPHER (ST. KITTS) AND NEVIS

The islands of St. Christopher, (popularly know as St. Kitts), and Nevis lie in the Leeward Island group in the eastern Caribbean. In 1983 it became a sovereign democratic federal state with Elizabeth II as head of state. St. Kitts consists of three extinct volcanoes linked by a sandy isthmus to other volcanic remains in the south. Around most of the island sugar cane is grown on the fertile soil covering the gentle slopes. Sugar is the chief export crop but market gardening and livestock rearing are being expanded on the steeper slopes about the cane fields. Industry includes sugar processing, brewing, distilling and bottling. St. Kitts has a major tourist development at Frigate Bay. Nevis, 3km south of St. Kitts, is an extinct volcano. Farming is declining here and tourism is now the main source of income.

Area : 261sq km (101sq mi)
Population : 43 410
Capital : Basseterre
Form of government :
Constitutional monarchy
Religions : Anglican, Methodist
Currency : East Caribbean
dollar

ST. LUCIA

St. Lucia is one of the Windward Islands in the Eastern Caribbean. It lies to the south of Martinique and to the north of St. Vincent. It was controlled alternatively by the French and the British for some two hundred years before becoming fully independant in 1979. St Lucia is an island of extinct volcanoes and the highest peak is 950m. In the west are the peaks of Pitons which rise directly from the sea to over 750m. The climate is wet tropical with a dry season from January to April. The economy depends on the the production of bananas and, to a lesser extent, coconuts. Production however is often affected by hurricanes, drought and disease. Tourism is becoming an important industry and Castries, the capital, is a popular calling point for cruise liners.

Area: 622sq km (240sq mi)
Population: 146 600
Capital: Castries
Form of government:
 Constitutional monarchy
Religion: RC
Currency: East Caribbean dollar

ST. VINCENT AND THE GRENADINES

St. Vincent is an island of the Lesser Antilles, situated in the Eastern Caribbean between St. Lucia and Grenada. St. Vincent is separated from Grenada by a chain of small islands known as the Grenadines. The largest of these small islands are Bequia, Mustique, Canouan, Mayrean and Union. The climate is tropical, with very heavy rain in the mountains. St. Vincent Island is mountainous and a chain of volcanoes runs up the middle of the island. Soufriere, 11234m, is active and its last eruption was in 1979. Farming is the main occupation on the island. Bananas for the UK are the main export and it is the world's leading producer of arrowroot starch. There is little manufacturing and the government is trying to promote tourism.

Area : 388sq km (150sq mi)
Population : 113 950
Capital : Kingstown
Form of government :
Constitutional monarchy
Religions : Anglican,
Methodist, RC
Currency : East Caribbean
dollar

SAN MARINO

San Marino is a tiny landlocked state in central Italy lying in the eastern foothills of the Apennines. It has wooded mountains and pasture land clustered around the limestone peaks of Monte Titano which rises to 739m. San Marino has a mild Mediterranean climate. The majority of the population work on the land or in forestry. Wheat, barley, maize and vines are grown and the main exports are wood machinery, chemical, wine, textiles, tiles, varnishes and ceramics. Some 3.5 million tourists visit the country each year and much of the country's revenue comes from the sale of stamps, postcards, souvenirs and duty free liquor. Italian currency is in general use but San Marino issues its own coins.

Area: 61sq km (24sq mi)
Population: 22 746
Capital: San Marino
Form of government: RC
Currency: Lira

SÃO TOMÉ AND PRÍNCIPE

São Tomé and Príncipe are volcanic islands which lie off the west coast of Africa. São Tomé is covered in extinct volcanic cones which reach 2024m at the highest peak. The coastal areas are hot and humid. Príncipe is a craggy island lying to the northeast of São Tomé. The climate is tropical with heavy rainfall from October to May. About 70% of the workforce work on the land, mainly in the state owned cocoa plantations. Small manufacturing industries include food processing and timber products

Area: 964sq km (372sq mi)
Population: 115 600
Capital: São Tomé
Form of government: Republic
Religion: RC
Currency: Dobra

SAUDI ARABIA

Saudi Arabia, which occupies over 70% of the Arabian Peninsula, is the largest Arab country by area. Over 95% of the country is desert and the largest expanse of sand in the world, "Rub'al-Khali", is found in the southeast of the country. In the west a narrow, humid coastal plain along the Red Sea is backed by steep mountains. The climate is hot with very little rain and some areas have no precipitation for years. The government has spent a considerable amount on reclamation of the desert for agriculture and the main products are dates, tomatoes, water melons and wheat, however the country's prosperity is based almost entirely on the exploitation of its vast reserves of oil and natural gas. Industries include petroleum refining, petrochemicals and fertilisers.

Area: 2 149 690sq km (829 995sq mi)
Population: 12 000 000
Capital: Riyadh
Other major cities: Mecca,
 Jeddah, Medina, Ta'if
Form of government: Monarchy
Religions: Sunni Islam,
Shia Islam
Currency: Rial

SENEGAL

Senegal is a former French colony in west Africa which extends from the most western point in Africa, Cape Verde, to the border with Mali. Senegal is mostly low lying and covered by Savanna. The Futa Jalon mountains in the south rise to 1515m. The climate is tropical with a dry season from October to June. The most densely populated region is in the southwest. Almost 80% of the labour force work in agriculture, growing ground nuts and cotton for export and millet, maize, rice and sorghum as subsistence crops. Senegal has been badly affected by the drought that has afflicted the Sahel and relies on food imports and international aid.

Area: 196 722sq km
(75 954sq mi)
Population: 7 170 000
Capital: Dakar
Other major cities: Thies,
Kaolack, St. Louis
Form of government:
Republic
Religions: Sunni Islam, RC
Currency: Franc CFA

SEYCHELLES

The Seychelles are a group of volcanic islands which lie in the western Indian Ocean about 1200km from the coast of east Africa. about forty of the islands are mountainous and consist of granite while just over fifty are coral islands. The climate is tropical maritime with heavy rain. About 90% of the people live on the island of Mahé which is the site of the capital, Victoria. The staple food is coconut, imported rice and fish. Tourism accounts for about 90% of the country's foreign exchange earnings and employs one-third of the labour force. The Seychelles are a one party socialist state and Soviet-made missiles have been installed as part of the islands' defence system.

Area: 280sq km (108sq mi)
Population: 67 378
Capital: Victoria
Form of government: Republic
Religion: RC
Currency: Seychelles rupee

SIERRA LEONE

Sierra Leone, on the Atlantic Coast of West Africa, is bounded by Guinea to the north and east and by Liberia to the south east. The coastal areas consist of wide swampy forested plains and these rise to a mountainous plateau in the east. The highest parts of the mountains are just under 2000m. The climate is tropical with a dry season from November to June. The main food of Sierra Leoneans is rice and this is grown in the swamplands at the coast. In the tropical forest areas, small plantations produce coffee, cocoa and oil palm. In the plateaux much forest has been cleared for growing of groundnuts. Most of the country's revenue comes from mining. Diamonds are panned from the rivers and there are deposits of iron ore, bauxite, rutile and some gold.

Area : 71 740sq km
(27 699sq mi)
Population : 4 140 000
Capital : Freetown
Form of government :
Republic
Religion : Animist,
Sunni Islam, Christian
Currency : Leone

SINGAPORE

Singapore, one of the world's smallest yet most successful countries, comprises 60 islands which are located at the foot of the Malay peninsula in southeast Asia. The main island, Singapore Island, is very low lying and the climate is hot and wet throughout the year. Only 3% of the land area is used for agriculture and most food is imported. It is self-sufficient in fish. Singapore has the largest oil refining centre in Asia. The country has a flourishing manufacturing industry for which it relies heavily on imports. Products include machinery and appliances, petroleum, food and beverages, chemicals, transport equipment, paper products and printing; and clothes. The Jurong Industrial Estate on the south of the island has over 1900 factories and employs 107 837 workers. Tourism is an important source of foreign revenue.

Area : 618sq km (239sq mi)
Population : 2 690 000
Capital : Singapore
Form of government :
Republic
Religions : Buddhist,
Sunni Islam, Christian
Currency : Singapore dollar

SOLOMON ISLANDS

The Solomon Islands lie in an area between 5° and 12° south of the equator to the east of Papua New Giunea, in the Pacific Ocean. The nation consists of six large islands and innumerable smaller ones. The larger islands are mountainous and covered in forests with rivers prone to flooding. Guada canal is the main island and the site of the capital, Honiara. The climate is hot and wet and typhoons are frequent. The main food crops grown are coconut, cassava, sweet potatoes, yams, taros and bananas. The forests are worked commercially and the fishing industry is developing with the help of the Japanese. Other industries include palm oil milling, fish canning and freezing, saw milling, food, tobacco and soft drinks.

Area : 28 896sq km
(11 157sq mi)
Population : 308 796
Capital : Honiara
Form of government :
Constitutional monarchy
Religions : Anglican, RC,
other Christian
Currency :
Solomon Island dollar

SOMALIA

Somalia is shaped like a large number seven and lies to the north of Africa's east coast. It is bounded north by the Gulf of Aden, south and east by the Indian Ocean and its neighbours include Djibouti, Ethiopia, and Kenya. The country is arid and most of it is low plateaux with scrub vegetation. Its two main rivers, the Juba and Shebelle, are used to irrigate crops. Most of the population live in the mountains and river valleys and there are a few towns on the coast. Main exports are live animals, meat, hides and skins. A few large scale banana plantations are found by the rivers. Years of drought have left Somalia heavily dependent on foreign aid and many of the younger population are emigrating to oil-rich Arab states.

Area : 637 657sq km
(246 199sq mi)
Population : 6 260 000
Capital : Mogadishu
Other major cities : Hargeisa,
Baidoa, Burao, Kismaayo
Form of government : Republic
Religion : Sunni Islam
Currency : Somali shilling

SOUTH AFRICA

The Republic of South Africa lies at the southern tip of the African continent and has a huge coastline on both the Atlantic and Indian Oceans. The country occupies a huge saucer shaped plateau, surrounding a belt of land which drops in steps to the sea. The rim of the saucer rises in the east, to 3482m, in the Drakensberg. In general the climate is healthy with plenty of sunshine and relatively low rainfall. This varies with latitude, distance from the sea and altitude. Of the total land area 58% is used as natural pasture. The main crops grown are maize, sorghum, wheat, groundnuts and sugarcane. A drought resistant variety of cotton is also now grown. It is South Africa's extraordinary mineral wealth which over shadows all its other natural resources. These include gold, coal, copper, iron ore, manganese and chrome ore.

Area : 1 221 037sq km (471 442sq mi)
Population : 30 190 000
Capital : Pretoria (Admin),
Capetown (Legis)
Other major cities. Johannesburg,
Durban, Port Elizabeth, Bloemfontein
Form of government : Republic
Religions : Dutch reformed,
Independent African, other Christian, Hindu
Currency : Rand

SPAIN

Spain is located in southwest Europe and occupies the greater part of the Iberian peninsula, which it shares with Portugal. It is a mountainous country, sealed off from the rest of Europe by the Pyrenees, which rise to over 3400m. Much of the country is a vast plateau, the Meseta Central, cut across by valleys and gorges. Its longest shoreline is the one that borders the Mediterranean Sea. Most of the country has a form of Mediterranean climate with mild moist winters and hot dry summers. Spain's principal agricultural products are cereals, vegetables and potatoes and large areas are under vines for the wine industry. Industry represents 72% of the country's export value and production includes textiles, paper, cement, steel and chemicals. Tourism is a major revenue earner, especially from the resorts on the east coast.

Area : 504 782sq km
(194 896sq mi)
Population : 39 540 000
Capital : Madrid
Other major cities : Barcelona,
Seville, Zaragosa, Malaga, Bilboa
Form of government : Constitutional monarchy
Religion : RC
Currency : Peseta

SRI LANKA

Sri Lanka is a teardrop shaped island in the Indian Ocean, lying south of the Indian peninsula from which it is separated by the Palk Strait. The climate is equatorial with a low annual temperature range but it is affected by both the northeast and southwest monsoons. Rainfall is heaviest in the southwest while the north and east are relatively dry. Agriculture engages 47% of the work force and the main crops are rice, tea, rubber and coconuts. Amongst the chief minerals mined and exported are precious and semiprecious stones. Graphite production is also important. The main industries are food, beverages and tobacco; textiles, clothing and leather goods, chemicals and plastics. Attempts are being made to increase revenue from tourism.

Area : 65 610sq km
(25 332sq mi)
Population : 16 810 000
Capital : Colombo
Other major cities : Dehiwela-
Mt.Lavinia, Moratuwa, Jaffna
Form of government : Republic
Religions : Buddhist, Hindu,
Christian, Sunni Islam
Currency : Sri Lankan Rupee

SUDAN

Sudan is the largest country in Africa, lying just south of the Tropic of Cancer in northeast Africa. The country covers much of the upper Hile basin and in the north the river winds through the Nubian and Libyan deserts forming a palm fringed strip of habitable land. The climate is tropical and temperatures are high throughout the year. In winter, nights are very cold. Rainfall increases in amount from north to south, the northern areas being virtually desert. Sudan is an agricultural country, subsistence farming accounting for 80% of production. Cotton is farmed commercially and accounts for about two-thirds of Sudan's exports. Sudan is the world's greatest source of gum Arabic used in medicines and inks. This is the only forest produce to be exported.

Area : 2 505 813sq km
(967 494sq mi)
Population : 25 560 000
Capital : Khartoum
Other major cities : Omdurman,
Khartoum North, Port Sudan
Form of government : Republic
Religions : Sunni Islam,
 Animist, Christian
Currency : Sudanese pound

SURINAME

Suriname is a republic in northeast South America,
bordered to the west by Guyana, to the east by Guiana
and to the south by Brazil. The country, formerly a
Dutch colony, declared independence in 1975.
Suriname comprises a swampy coastal plain, a forested
central plateau and southern mountains. The climate is
tropical with heavy rainfall. Temperatures at
Paramaribo average 26-27°C all year round. Rice and
sugar are farmed on the coastal plains but the mining
of bauxite is what the economy depends on. This
makes up 80% of exports. Suriname has resources of
oil and timber but these are so far underexploited. The
country is politically very unstable and in need of
financial aid to develop these resources.

Area : 163 265sq km (63 037sq mi)
Population : 416 839
Capital : Paramaribo
Form of government : Republic
Religions : Hindu, RC,
Sunni Islam
Currency : Suriname guilder

SWAZILAND

Swaziland is a landlocked hilly enclave almost entirely within the borders of the Republic of South Africa. The mountains in the west of the country rise to almost 2000m, then descend in steps of savanna towards hilly country in the east. The climate is subtropical moderated by altitude. The land between 400m and 850m is planted with orange groves and pineapple fields, while on the lower land sugar cane flourishes in irrigated areas. Asbestos is mined in the northwest of the country. Manufacturing includes, fertilisers, textiles, leather and tableware. Swaziland attracts a lot of tourists from South Africa mainly to its spas and casinos.

Area : 17 36sq km (6 704sq mi)
Population : 681 059
Capital : Mbabane
Other major cities : Manzini,
Big Bend, Mhlume
Form of government :
Monarchy
Religion : Christian, Animist
Currency : Emalangeni

SWEDEN

Sweden is a large country in northern Europe which makes up half of the Scandinavian peninsula. It stretches from the Baltic Sea north, to well within the Arctic Circle. The south is generally flat, the north mountainous and along the coast there are 20 000 or more islands and islets. Summers are warm but short and winters are long and cold. In the north snow may lie for four to seven months. Dairy farming is the predominant agricultural activity. Only 7% of Sweden is cultivated with the emphasis on fodder crops, grain and sugar beet. About 57% of the country is covered in forest and the sawmill, wood pulp and paper industries are all of great importance. Sweden is one of the world's leading producers of iron ore most of which is extracted from within the Arctic Circle. Other principal industries are engineering and electrical goods, motor vehicles and furniture making.

Area : 449 964sq km (173 731sq mi)
Population : 8 500 000
Capital : Stockholm
Other major cities : Goteborg,
Malmo, Uppsala, Orebro
Form of government :
Constitutional monarchy
Religion : Lutheran
Currency : Krona

SWITZERLAND

Switzerland is a landlocked country in central Europe sharing its borders with France, Italy, Austria, Liechtenstein and Germany. The Alps occupy the southern half of the country, forming two main east-west chains, divided by the rivers, Rhine and Rhone. The climate is either continental or mountain type. Summers are generally warm and winters cold and both are affected by altitude. Northern Switzerland is the industrial part of the country and where its most important cities are located. Basle is famous for its pharmaceuticals and Zurich for electrical engineering and machinery. It is also in this region that the famous cheeses, clocks, watches and chocolates are produced. Switzerland has huge earnings from international finance and tourism.

Are : 41 293sq km (15 943sq mi)
Population : 6 700 000
Capital : Berne
Other major cities : Zurich, Basle, Geneva, Lausanne
Form of government : Federal state
Religions : RC, Protestant
Currency : Swiss franc

SYRIA

Syria is a country in southwest Asia which borders on the Mediterranean Sea in the west. Much of the country is mountainous behind the narrow fertile coastal plain. The eastern region is desert or semi-desert, a stony inhospitable land. The coast has a Mediterranean climate with hot dry summers and mild wet winters. About 50% of the workforce get their living from agriculture, sheep, goats and cattle are raised and cotton, barley, wheat, tobacco, fruit and vegetables are grown. Reserves of oil are small compared to neighbouring Iraq but it has enough to make the country self-sufficient and provide three-quarters of the nations export earnings. Industries such as textiles, leather, chemicals and cement have developed rapidly in the last 20 years.

Area : 185 180sq km
(71 4948sq mi)
Population : 11 300 000
Capital : Damascus
other major cities : Aleppo,
Homs, Lattakia, Hama
Form of government : Republic
Religion : Sunni Islam
Currency : Syrian pound

TAIWAN

Taiwan is an island which straddles the Tropic of Cancer in East Asia. It lies about 160km off the southeast coast of mainland China. It is predominantly mountainous in the interior, the tallest peak rising to 3997m at Yusham. The climate is warm and humid for most of the year. Winters are mild and summers rainy. The soils are fertile and a wide range of crops including tea, rice, sugar cane and bananas are grown. Taiwan is a major international trading nation with some of the most successful export processing zones in the world, accommodating domestic and overseas companies. Exports include machinery, electronics, textiles, footwear, toys and sporting goods.

Area : 36 179sq km
(13 969sq mi)
Population : 20 300 000
Capital : Taipei
Other major cities : Kaohsiung,
Taichung, Tainan
Form of government : Republic
Religions : Taoist, Buddhist,
Christian
Currency : New Taiwan dollar

TANZANIA

Tanzania lies on the east coast of central Africa and comprises a large mainland area and the islands of Pembar and Zanzibar. The mainland consists mostly of plateaux broken by mountainous areas and the east African section of the Great Rift Valley. The climate is very varied and is controlled largely by altitude and distance from the sea. The coast is hot and humid, the central plateau drier and the mountains semi-temperate. 80% of Tanzanians make a living from the land but productivity is low and there is no surplus from the crops, mainly maize, they grow. Cash crops include cotton and coffee. The islands are more successful agriculturally and have important coconut and clove plantations. Tanzania's mineral resources are limited and of low grade and there are few manufacturing industries.

Area : 945 087sq km (364 898sq mi)
Population : 24 800 000
Capital : Dodoma
Other major cities : Dar es Salaam,
Zanzibar, Mwanza, Tanga
Form of government : Republic
Religions : Sunni Islam, RC,
Anglican, Hindu
Currency : Tanzanian shilling

THAILAND

Thailand, a country about the same size as France located in southeast Asia, is a tropical country of mountains and jungles, rain forests and green plains. Central Thailand is a densely populated, fertile plain and the mountainous Isthmus of Kra joins southern Thailand to Malaysia. Thailand has a subtropical climate with heavy monsoon rains from June to October, a cool season from October to March and a hot season from March to June. The central plain of Thailand contains vast expanses of paddy fields which produce enough rice to rank Thailand as the world's leading exporter. The narrow southern peninsula is very wet and it is here that rubber is produced. Thailand is the world's third largest exporter of rubber.

Area ; 513 115sq km (198 114sq mi)
Population : 55 900 00
Capital : Bangkok
Other major cities : Chiang Mia, Songkhla, Hat Yaí
Form of government : Constitutional monarchy
Religions : Buddhist, Sunni Islam
Currency : Baht

TOGO

Togo is a tiny country with a narrow coastal plain on the Gulf of Guinea in west Africa. Grassy plains in the north and south are separated by the Togo Highlands, which run from southwest to northeast and rise to nearly 1000m. High plateaux, mainly in the more southerly ranges, are heavily forested with teak, mahogany and bamboo. Over 80% of the population are involved in agriculture with yams and millet as the principal crops. Coffee, cocoa and cotton are grown for cash. Minerals, especially phosphates, are now the main export earners. Togo's exports are suffering from the recession in its major markets in western Europe.

Area : 56 785sq km
(21 925sq mi)
Population : 3 400 000
Capital : Lome
Form of government :
Republic
Religions : Animist, RC,
Sunni Islam
Currency : Franc CFA

TONGA

Tonga is situated about 20° south of the equator and just west of the International Date Line in the Pacific Ocean. It comprises over 170 islands and only about one-fifth of them are inhabited. It comprises a low limestone chain of islands in the east and a higher volcanic chain in the west. The climate is warm with heavy rainfall. The government owns all the land and males can rent an allotment for growing food. Yams, cassava and taro are grown as subsistence crops and fish from the sea supplements their diet. Bananas and coconuts are grown for export. The main industry is coconut processing.

Area : 750sq km (290sq mi)
Population : 95 200
Capital : Nukulalofa
Form of government :
Constitutional monarchy
Religions : Methodist, RC
Currency : Pa'anga

TRINIDAD AND TOBAGO

Trinidad and Tobago form the third largest commonwealth country in the West Indies and are situated off the Orinoco Delta in northeastern Venezuela. The islands are the most southerly of the Lesser Antilles. Trinidad consists of a mountainous Northern Range in the north and undulating plains in the south. Tobago is more mountainous. The climate is tropical with little variation in temperatures throughout the year and a rainy season from June to December. Trinidad is one of the oldest oil producing countries in the world. Output is small but provides 90% of Trinidad's exports. Sugar, coffee and cocoa are grown for export but imports of food now account for 10% of total imports. Tobago depends mainly on tourism to make a living.

Area 5 130sq km (1 981sq mi)
Population : 1 240 000
Capital : Port of Spain
Form of government : Republic
Religions : RC, Hindu,
Anglican, Sunni Islam
Currency : Trinidad and Tobago
dollar

TUNISIA

Tunisia is a North African country which lies on the south coast of the Mediterranean Sea. It's bounded by Algeria to the west and Libya to the south. Northern Tunisia consists of hills, plains and valleys. Inland mountains separate the coastal zone from the central plains before the land drops down to an area of salt pans and the Sahara Desert. Climate ranges from warm temperate in the north, to desert in the south. 40% of the population are engaged in agriculture producing wheat, barley, olives, tomatoes, dates and citrus fruits. The mainstay of Tunisia's modern economy, however, is oil from the Sahara, phosphates and tourism on the Mediterranean coast.

Area : 163 610sq km
(63 170sq mi)
Population : 7 750 000
Capital : Tunis
Other major cities : Sfax,
Bizera, Djerba
Form of government :
Republic
Religion : Sunni Islam
Currency : Tunisian dinar

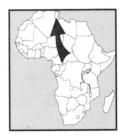

TURKEY

With land on the continents of Europe and Asia, Turkey forms a bridge between the two. It guards the sea passage between the Mediterranean and the Black Sea. Only 5% of its area, Thrace, is in Europe and the much larger area, known as Anatolia, is in Asia. European Turkey is fertile agricultural land with a Mediterranean climate. Asiatic Turkey is bordered to the north by the Pontus Mountains and to the south by the Taurus Mountains. The climate here ranges from Mediterranean to hot summers and bitterly cold winters in the central plains. Agriculture employs over half the workforce. Major crops are wheat, rice, tobacco and cotton. Manufacturing industry includes iron and steel, textiles, motor vehicles and Turkey's famous carpets. Hydro electric power is supplied by the Tigris and Euphrates. Tourism is a fast developing industry.

Area : 779 452sq km
(300 946sq mi)
Population : 50 670 000
Capital : Ankara
Other major cities : Istanbul,
Izmir, Adana, Bursa
Form of government : Republic
Religion : Sunni Islam
Currency : Turkish lira

TUVALU

Tuvalu is located just north of Fiji, in the South Pacific, and consists of nine coral Atholls. The group were formerly known as the Ellice Islands and the main island and capital is Finafuti. The climate is tropical with temperatures averaging 30°C and annual rainfall ranges from 3000mm to 4000mm. Coconut palms are the main crop and fruit and vegetables are grown for local consumption. Sea fishing is extremely good and although largely unexploited, licences have been granted to Japan, Taiwan and South Korea to fish the local waters. Most export revenue comes from the sail of elaborate postage stamps to philatelists.

Area : 26sq km (10sq mi)
Population : 8 229
Capital : Funa Futi
Form of government :
Constitutional monarchy
Religion : Protestant
Currency : Australian dollar

UGANDA

Uganda is a landlocked country in east central Africa. The equator runs through the south of the country and for most part it is a richly fertile land, well watered, with a kindly climate. In the west are the Ruivenzori Mountains, which rise to over 5000m and are snow capped. The lowlands around Lake Victoria, once forested, have now mostly been cleared for cultivation. Agriculture employs over three-quarters of the labour and the main crops grown for subsistence are plantains, cassava and sweet potatoes. Coffee is the main cash crop and accounts for 90% of the county's exports. Attempts are being made to expand the tea plantations in the west, develop a copper mine and introduce new industries to Kampala the capital.

Area : 235 880sq km
(91 073sq mi)
Population : 17 000 000
Capital : Kampala
Other major cities : Jinja,
Masaka, Mbale
Religions : RC, Protestant,
Animist, Sunni Islam
Currency : Uganda shilling

UNITED ARAB EMIRATES

The United Arab Emirates is a federation of seven oil rich sheikdoms located in The Gulf. As well as its main coast on the Gulf, the country has a short coast on the Gulf of Oman. The land is mainly flat sandy desert except to the north on the peninsula where the Hajar Mountains rise to 2081m. The summers are hot and humid with temperatures reaching 49°C but from October to May the weather is warm and sunny with pleasant, cool evenings. The only fertile areas are the emirate of Ras al Khaymah, the coastal plain of Al Fujayrah and the oases. Abu Dhabi and Dubai are the main industrial centres and using their wealth from the oil industry they are now diversifying industry by building aluminium smelters, cement factories and steel rolling mills. Dubai is the richest state in the world.

Area : 83 600sq km
(32 278sq mi)
Population : 1 600 000
Capital : Abu Dhabi
Other major cities : Dubai,
Sharjh, Ras al Khaimah
Religion : Sunni Islam
Currency : Dirham

UNITED KINGDOM

Situated in northwest Europe, the United Kingdom of Great Britain and Northern Ireland, comprises the island of Great Britain and the northeast of Ireland. The south and east of Britain is low lying, and the Pennines form a backbone running through northern England. Scotland has the largest area of upland, and Wales is a highland block. Northern Ireland has a few hilly areas. The climate is cool temperate with mild conditions and an even annual rainfall. The principal crops are wheat, barley, sugar beet, fodder crops and potatoes. Livestock includes cattle, sheep, pigs and poultry. Fishing is important off the east coast. The UK is primarily an industrial country, although the recent recession has left high unemployment and led to the decline of some of the older industries such as coal, textiles and heavy engineering. A growing industry is electronics, much of it defence-related.

Area : 244 100sq km (94 247sq mi)
Population : 57 240 000
Capital : London
Other major cities : Birmingham, Manchester, Glasgow,Liverpool
Form of government :
Constitutional monarchy
Religion : Anglican, RC, Presbyterian, Methodist
Currency : Pound sterling

UNITED STATES OF AMERICA

The USA stretches across central north America, from the Atlantic Ocean in the east, to the Pacific Ocean in the west and from Canada in the north, to Mexico and the Gulf of Mexico in the south. It consists of fifty states, including Alaska in northwest Canada and Hawaii in the Pacific Ocean. The climate varies in such a large country. In Alaska there are polar conditions and in the Gulf coast and in Florida conditions may be subtropical . Although agricultural production is high it employs only 1.5% of the population due primarily to its advanced technology. The USA is a world leader in oil production. The main industries are iron and steel, chemicals, motor vehicles, aircraft, telecommunications equipment, computers, electronics and textiles. The USA is the richest and most powerful nation in the world.

Area : 9 372 614sq km (3 618 766sq mi)
Population : 249 630 000
Capital : Washington DC.
Other major cities : New York,
Los Angeles, Chicago, Houston,
Philadelphia, San Diego, Detroit
Form of government : Federal Republic
Religion : Protestant, RC, Judaism, Eastern Orthodox
Currency : US dollar

URUGUAY

Uruguay is one of the smallest countries in South America. It lies on the east coast of the continent, to the south of Brazil, and is bordered to the west by the Uruguay river, Rio de la Plata to the south and the Atlantic Ocean to the east. The country consists of low plains and plateaux. In the southeast hills rise to 500m. About 90% of the land is suitable for agriculture but only 10% is cultivated, the remainder being used to graze vast herds of cattle and sheep. The cultivated land is made up of vineyards, rice fields and groves of olives and citrus fruits. Uruguay has only one major city in which half the population live. The country has no mineral resources, oil or gas but has built hydro electric power stations at Palmar and Salto Grande.

Area : 177 414sq km
(68 500sq mi)
Population : 3 100 000
Capital : Montevideo
form of government : Republic
Religions : RC, Protestant
Currency : Uruguayan Nuevo
peso

VANUATU

Vanuatu, formerly known as the New Hebrides, is located in the western Pacific, southeast of the Solomon Islands and about 1750km east of Australia. About eighty islands ,make up the group. Some of the islands are mountainous and include active volcanoes. The largest islands are Espírtu Santo, Malekula and Afate, on which the capital Vila is sited. Vanuatu has a tropical climate which is moderated by the southeast trade winds from May to October. The majority of the labour force are engaged in subsistence farming and the main exports include copra, fish and cocoa. Tourism is becoming an important industry.

Area : 12 189sq km
(4 706sq mi)
Population : 142 630
Capital : Vila
Form of government :
Republic
Religion : Protestant,
Animist
Currency : Vatu

VATICAN CITY STATE

The Vatican City State lies in the heart of Rome on a low hill on the west bank of the river Tiber. It is the world's smallest independent state and headquarters of the Roman Catholic Church. It is a walled city made up of the Vatican Palace, the Papal Gardens, St. Peter's Square and St. Peter's Basilica. The state has its own police, newspaper, coinage, stamps and radio station. The radio station "Radio Vaticana" broadcasts a service in thirty four languages from transmitters within the Vatican City. Its main tourist attractions are the frescoes of the Sistine Chapel painted by Michelangelo Buonarroti. The Pope exercises sovereignty and has absolute legislative, executive and judicial powers.

Area : 44 hectares (108.7 acres)
Population : 1 000
Capital : Vatican City
Form of government :
Papal commission
Religion : RC
Currency : Vatican City lira

VIETNAM

Vietnam is a long narrow country in southeast Asia which runs down the coast of the South China Sea. It has a narrow central area which links broader plains centred on the Red and Mekong rivers. The narrow zone, known as Annam, is hilly and makes communications between north and south difficult. The climate is humid with tropical conditions in the south and subtropical in the north. The far north can be very cold when polar air blows over Asia. Agriculture employs over three-quarters of the labour force. The main crop is rice but cassava, maize and sweet potatoes are also grown for domestic consumption. Rubber, tea and coffee are grown for export. Major industries are food processing, textiles, cement, cotton and silk manufacture, however Vietnam remains underdeveloped.

Area : 331 689sq km (128 065sq mi)
Population : 65 000 000
Capital : Hanoi
Other major cities :
Ho Chi Minh City, Haiphong
Form of government : Socialist
republic
Religion : Buddhist, Taoist, RC
Currency : Dong

VENEZUELA

Venezuela forms the northern most crest of South America. Its northern coast lies along the Caribbean Sea and it is bounded to the west by Columbia and to the southeast and south by Guyana and Brazil. In the northwest a spur of the Andes runs southwest to northeast. The river Orinoco cuts the country in two, and north of the river run the undulating plains known as the Llanos. South of the river are the Guiana Highlands. The climate ranges from warm temperate to tropical. Temperatures vary little throughout the year and rainfall is plentiful. In the Llanos area cattle are herded across the plains and this region makes the country almost self-sufficient in meat. Sugar cane and coffee are grown for export but petroleum and gas account for 95% of export earnings. The oil fields lie in the northwest near lake Maracaibo, where there are over 10 000 oil derricks.

Area : 912 050sq km (352 143sq mi)
Population : 9 250 000
Capital : Caracas
Other major cities : Maracaibo,
Valencia, Barquisimeto
Form of government : Federal
republic
Religion : RC
Currency : Bolívar

WESTERN SAMOA

Western Samoa lies in the Polynesian sector of the Pacific Ocean, about 720km northeast of Fiji. It consists of seven small islands and two larger volcanic islands, Savai'i and Upolu. Savai'i is largely covered with volcanic peaks and lava plateaux. Upolu is home to two-thirds of the population and the capital Apia. The climate is tropical with high temperatures and very heavy rainfall. The islands have been fought over by the Dutch, British, Germans and Americans but they now lead the lifestyle of traditional Polynesians. Subsistence agriculture is the main activity and copra, cocoa and bananas are the main exports. Many tourists visit the grave of Robert Louis Stevenson whose home is now the official home of the king.

Area : 2 831sq km
(1 093sq mi)
Population : 163 000
Capital : Apia
Form of government :
Constitutional monarchy
Religion : Protestant
Currency : Tala

YEMEN

Yemen is bounded by Saudi Arabia in the north, Oman in the east, the Gulf of Aden in the south and the Red Sea in the west. The country was formed after the unification of the previous Yemen Arab Republic and the People's Democratic Republic of Yemen in 1989. Most of the country comprises rugged mountains and trackless desert lands. The country is almost entirely dependant on agriculture even though a very small percentage is fertile. The main crops are coffee, cotton, millet, sorghum and fruit. Fishing is an important industry. Other industry is on a very small scale. There are textile factories, and plastic, rubber and aluminium goods, paints and matches are produced. Modernisation of industry is slow due to lack of funds.

Area : 195 000sq km
(75 290sq mi)
Population : 12 000 000
Capital : Sana'a,
Commercial Capital : Aden
Form of government : Republic
Religion : Zaidist, Shia Islam,
Sunni Islam
Currency : Riyal and dinar

YUGOSLAVIA

A federal republic of south-east Europe. It was created in 1918, and became a single republic after the Second World War under the Communist leadership of Marshal Tito. The six constituent republics were Serbia, Slovenia, Croatia, Montenegro, Macedonia and Bosnia Herzegovina. Serbia was always the dominant republic, and the seat of the capital, Belgrade. In 1991 Slovenia and Croatia became independent, and Bosnia and Macedonia may follow suit. The economy is largely agricultural, but exports include chemicals, machinery, textiles and clothing. The main languages are Serbo-Croat and Macedonian. (255 804 sq km/98 766 sq mi; pop. 23 000 000; cur. Yugoslav dinar = 100 paras)

Serbia a land-locked republic, and the largest republic of Yugoslavia. The capital is Belgrade (88 361 sq km/ 34 107 sq mi; pop. 9 314 000)

Slovenia a republic bordering Austria, Hungary, Italy and Croatia, which declared independence from Yugoslavia in 1991. The capital is Ljubljana. (20 251 sq km/7817 sq mi; pop. 1 891 900)

Croatia a former republic of Yugoslavia which became an independent state in 1991. The capital is Zagreb. (56 538 sq km/21 824 sq mi; pop. 4 601 500)

Montenegro the smallest of the republics of Yugoslavia, in the south-west on the Adriatic Sea and bordering Albania. The capital is Titograd. (13 812 sq km/5331 sq mi; pop. 584 300)

Macedonia the most southerly of the republics of Yugoslavia, with Skopje as its capital. (25 713 sq km/9928 sq mi; pop. 1 912 200)

Bosnia Herzegovina one of the six former republics of Yugoslavia. In 1991 it declared its intention to become an independent state. The capital is Sarajevo. (51 129 sq km/19 736 sq mi; pop. 4 124 000)

ZAÏRE

Situated in west central Africa, Zaïre is a vast country with a short coastline of only 40km on the Atlantic Ocean. Rain forests which cover about 55% of the country, contain valuable hardwoods such as mahogany and ebony. The country is drained by the river Zaïre and its main tributaries. Mountain ranges and plateaux surround the Zaïre Basin and in the east the Puwenzori Mountains overlook the lakes in the Great Rift Valley. In the central region the climate is hot and wet all year but elsewhere there are well marked wet and dry seasons. Agriculture employs 75% of the population yet less than 3% of the country can be cultivated. Grazing land is limited by the infestation of the Tsetse fly. Cassava is the main subsistence crop and coffee, tea, cocoa, rubber and palms are grown for export. Minerals, mainly copper, cobalt, zinc and diamonds, account for 60% of exports.

Area : 2 345 409sq km
 (905 562sq mi)
Population : 34 140 000
Capital : Kinshasa
Other major cities : Lubumbashi,
Mbuji-Mayi, Kananga,
Form of government : Republic
Religion : RC, Protestant, Animist
Currency : Zaïre

ZAMBIA

Zambia, situated in Central Africa, is made up of high plateaux. Bordering it to the south is the Zambesi river and in the southwest it borders on the Kalahari Desert. It has some other large rivers, including the Luangwa, and lakes, the largest of which is Lake Bangwenlu. The climate is tropical, modified somewhat by altitude. The country has a wide range of wildlife and there are large game parks on the Luangwa and Kajue rivers, Agriculture is underdeveloped and most food stuffs have to be imported. Zambia's economy relies heavily on the mining of copper, lead, zinc and cobalt. The poor market prospects for copper, which will eventually be exhausted, make it imperative for Zambia to develop her vast agricultural potential.

Area : 752 614sq km
(290 584sq mi)
Population : 8 500 000
Capital : Lusaka
Other major cities : Kitwe,
 Ndola, Mujulira
Form of government : Republic
Religion : Christian, Animist
Currency : Kwacha

ZIMBABWE

Zimbabwe is a landlocked country in Southern Africa. It is a country with spectacular physical features and is teeming with wildlife. It is bordered in the north by the Zambesi river, which flows over the mile wide Victoria Falls before entering Lake Kariba. In the south, the river Lumpopo marks its border with South Africa. Most of the country is over 300m above sea level and a great plateau between 1200m and 1500m occupies the central area. Massive granite outcrops called kopjes also dot the landscape. The climate is tropical in the lowlands and subtropical in the higher land. About 75% of the labour force are employed in agriculture. Tobacco, sugar cane, cotton, wheat and maize are exported and form the basis of processing industries. Tourism is a major growth industry.

Area : 390 580sq km
(150 803sq mi)
Population : 9 370 000
Capital : Harare
Other major cities : Bulawayo,
Mutare, Gweru
Form of government : Republic
Religion : Animist, Anglican,
RC
Currency : Zimbabwe dollar

MAPS
of
THE WORLD

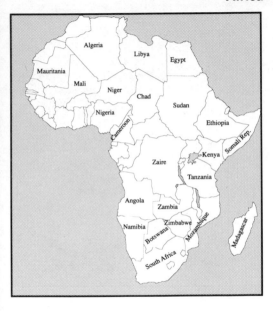

North America

Alaska
(USA)

Canada

USA

Mexico

Central America

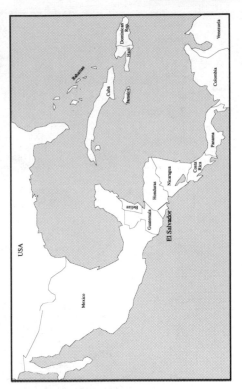

South America

Australasia

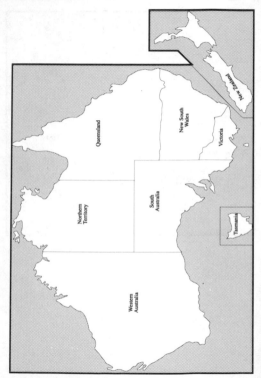

Queensland

New South Wales

Victoria

Northern Territory

South Australia

Western Australia

New Zealand

Tasmania

Europe

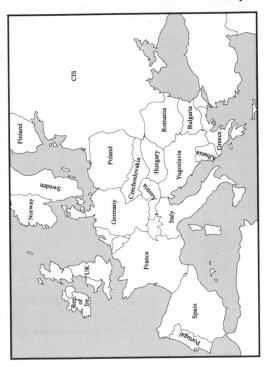

- CIS
- Finland
- Sweden
- Norway
- Poland
- Czechoslovakia
- Germany
- Hungary
- Austria
- Romania
- Bulgaria
- Greece
- Albania
- Yugoslavia
- Italy
- France
- UK
- Rep. of Ire.
- Spain
- Portugal

Northern Europe

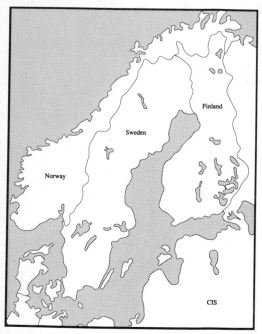

Southern Europe

France
Italy
Romania
Yugoslavia
Bulgaria
Alb.
Greece
Turkey
Tunisia
Algeria
Libya
Egypt

Mediterranean

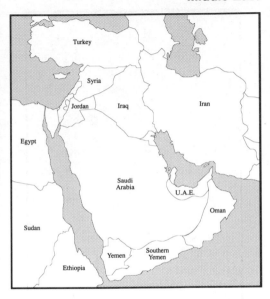

The World

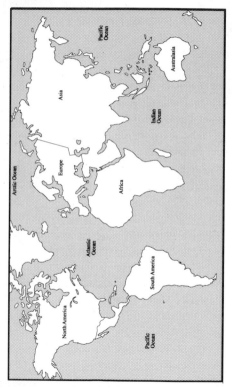

Pacific Ocean

Australasia

Asia

Indian Ocean

Arctic Ocean

Europe

Africa

Atlantic Ocean

South America

North America

Pacific Ocean

EARTH'S
STATISTICS

Earth's Vital Statistics

Age: Approx 4600 million years.

Weight: Approx 5.976 x 10^{21} tonnes

Diameter: Pole to Pole through the centre of the Earth 12 713 km (7900 miles);across the Equator through the centre of the Earth 12 756 km (7926 miles).

Circumference: Around the Poles 40 008 km (24 861 miles); around the Equator 40 091 km (24 912 miles)

Area: Land 148 326 000sq km (57 268 700sq miles) – 29% of total surface; Water 361 740 000sq km (139 667 810sq miles) – 71% of total surface

Volume: 1 084 000 million cubic km (260 160 million cubic miles)

Volume of the oceans: 1321 million cubic km (317 million cubic miles)

Average height of land: 840m (2756ft) above sea level

Average depth of ocean:	3808m (12 493ft) below sea level.
Density:	5.52 times water
Mean temperature:	22°C (72°F)
Length of year:	365.25 days
Length of one rotation:	23 hours 56 minutes
Mean distance from Sun:	149 600 000 km (92,960,000 miles)
Mean velocity in orbit:	29.8 km (18.5 miles) per second
Escape velocity:	11.2 km (6.96 miles) per second
Atmosphere:	Main constituents: nitrogen (78.5%), oxygen (21%)
Crust:	Main constituents: oxygen (47%), silicon (28%), aluminium (8%), iron (5%).
Known satellites:	One

Deserts

	sq km	sq miles
Sahara	9,065,000	3,500,000
Australian Desert	1,550,000	598,455
Arabian Desert	1,300,000	501,930
Gobi Desert	1,295,000	500,000
Kalahari	520,000	200,772

Oceans

	Max. Depth		Area	
	metres	feet	sq km	sq miles
Pacific	11 033	36 197	165,384,000	63,860,000
Atlantic	8 381	27 496	82,217,000	31,744,000
Indian	8 047	26 401	73,481,000	28,371,000
Arctic	5 450	17 880	14,056,000	5,427,000

Largest Islands

Islands (location)	Population	Area (sq km)	(sq miles)
Greenland (N. Atlantic)	55,000	2,175,600	840,000
New Guinea (S.W. Pacific)	4,528,682	808,510	312,166
Borneo (S.W. Pacific)	11,263,087	751,900	290,309
Madagascar (Indian Ocean)	11,238,000	587,041	226,657
Baffin I. (Canadian Arctic)	8,298	476,070	183,811
Sumatra (Indian Ocean)	36,881,990	473,607	182,860
Honshu (N.W. Pacific)	98,352,000	230,455	88,979
Great Britain (N. Atlantic)	54,285 422	229,880	88,757
Victoria I. (Canadian Arctic)	1,410	212,695	82,122
Ellesmere (Canadian Arctic)	54	212,690	82,120

Principal Mountains of The World

Name *(location)*	Height *(m)*	Height *(ft)*
Everest		
(Tibet-Nepal)	8,848	29,028
Godwin-Austen or K2		
(India)	8,611	28,250
Kangchenjunga		
(Nepal-India)	8,587	28,170
Makalu		
(Nepal)	8,464	27,766
Dhaulagiri		
(Nepal)	8,168	26,795
Nanga Parbat		
(India)	8,125	26,657
Gosainthan		
(Tibet)	8,012	26,286
Nanda Devi		
(India)	7,816	25,643
Kamet		
(India)	7,756	25,446

Name (location)	Height (m)	Height (ft)
Namcha Barwa (Tibet)	7,756	25,446
Gurla Mandhata (Tibet)	7,729	25,355
Kongur (China)	7,720	25,325
Tirich Mir (Pakistan)	7,691	25,230
Minya Kanka (China)	7,556	24,790
Kula Kangri (Tibet)	7,555	24,784
Muztagh Ata (China)	7,546	24,757
Kommunizma (Tadzhik S.S.R.)	7,495	24,590
Pobedy (USSR-China)	7,439	24,406
Chomo Lhari (Bhutan-Tibet)	7,313	23,992

Name (location)	Height (m)	Height (ft)
Api (Nepal)	7,132	23,399
Lenina (Kirghiz S.S.R.-Tadzhik S.S.R.)	7,134	23,405
Acongagua (volcano) (Argentina)	6,960	22,834
Ojos del Salado (Argentina)	6,908	22,664
Tupungato (Argentina-Chile)	6,801	22,310
Mercedario (Argentina)	6,770	22,211
Huascarán (Peru)	6,769	22,205
Llullailaco (Chile)	6,723	22,057
Neradas de Cachi (Argentina)	6,720	22,047
Kailas (Tibet)	6,714	22,027

Name (location)	Height (m)	Height (ft)
Incahuasi (Argentina)	6,709	22,011
Tengri Khan (Kirghiz S.S.R.)	6,695	21,965
Sajama (Bolivia)	6,542	21,463
Illampu (Bolivia)	6,485	21,276
Antofalla (volcanic) (Argentina)	6,441	21,129
Illimani (Bolivia)	6,402	21,004
Chimborazo (volcanic) (Ecuador)	6,310	20,702
Cumbre de la Mejicana (Argentina)	6,249	20,500
McKinley (Alaska)	6,194	20,320
Copiapo or Azifre (Chile)	6,080	19,947

Name (location)	Height (m)	Height (ft)
Logan (Yukon, Canada)	6,050	19,849
Cotopaxi (volcanic) (Ecuador)	5,897	19,344
Kilimanjaro (volcanic) (Tanzania)	5,895	19,340
Ollagüe (Chile-Bolivia)	5,868	19,250
Cerro del Potro (Argentina-Chile)	5,830	19,127
Misti (volcanic) (Peru)	5,822	19,101
Cayambe (Ecuador)	5,797	19,016
Huila (volcanic) (Colombia)	5,750	18,865
Citlaltepi (Mexico)	5,699	18,697
Demavend (Iran)	5,664	18,582

Name *(location)*	Height *(m)*	Height *(ft)*
Elbrus (volcanic) (Georgian S.S.R.)	5,633	18,481
St. Elias (volcanic) (Alaska, Canada)	5,489	18,008
Popocatepetl (volcanic) (Mexico)	5,453	17,888
Cerro Lejfa (Chile)	5,360	17,585
Foraker (Alaska)	5,304	17,400
Maipo (volcanic) (Argentina-Chile)	5,290	17,355
Ixtaccihuati (volcanic) (Mexico)	5,286	17,342
Lucania (Yukon, Canada)	5,228	17,150
Tomila (volcanic) (Colombia)	5,215	17,109
Dykh Tau (European R.S.F.S.R.)	5,203	17,070

Name (location)	Height (m)	Height (ft)
Kenya (Kenya)	5,200	17,058
Ararat (Turkey)	5,165	16,945
Vinson Massif (Antarctica)	5,139	16,860
Kazbek (volcanaic) (Georgian S.S.R.)	5,047	16,558
Blackburn (Alaska)	5,037	16,523
Jaya (Irian Jaya, Indonesia)	5,030	16,502
Sanford (Alaska)	4,941	16,208
Klyucheveyskava (volcanic) (Khabarovsk Territory, C.I.S.)	4,750	15,584
Mont Blanc (France-Italy)	4,807	15,771
Domuyo (volcanic) (Argentina)	4,800	15,748

Name (location)	Height (m)	Height (ft)
Vancouver		
(Alaska-Yukon, Canada)	4,786	15,700
Trikora		
(West Irian, Indonesia)	4,750	15,584
Fairweather		
(Alaska-British Colombia, Canada)	4,670	15,320
Monte Rosa		
(Switzerland-Italy)	4,634	15,203
Ras Dashan		
(Ethiopia)	4,621	15,158
Belukha		
(Kazak S.S.R.)	4,506	14,783
Markham		
(Antartica)	4,350	14,271
Meru (volcanic)		
(Tanzania)	4,566	14,979
Hubbard		
(Alaska-Yukon)	4,557	14,950
Kirkpatrick		
(Antarctica)	4,528	14,855

Name (location)	Height (m)	Height (ft)
Karisimbi (volcanic) (Rwanda-Zaire)	4,508	14,787
Weisshorn (Switzerland)	4,505	14,780
Matterhorn/Mont Cervin (Switzerland-Italy)	4,478	14,690
Whitney (California)	4,419	14,495
Elbert (Colorado)	4,399	14,431
Massive Mount (Colorado)	4,397	14,424
Harvard (Colorado)	4,396	14,420
Rainier or Tacoma (Washington)	4,392	14,408
Williamson (California)	4,382	14,375
La Plata (Colorado)	4,371	14,340

Name (location)	Height (m)	Height (ft)
Blanca Peak (Colorado)	4,364	14,317
Uncompahgre (Colorado)	4,361	14,306
Crestone (Colorado)	4,356	14,291
Lincoln (Colorado)	4,354	14,284
Grays (Colorado)	4,351	14,274
Evans (Colorado)	4,347	14,260
Longs (Colorado)	4,345	14,255
White (California)	4,343	14,246
Colima (volcanic) (Mexico)	4,340	14,236
Shavano (Colorado)	4,337	14,229

Name (location)	Height (m)	Height (ft)
Princeton (Colorado)	4,327	14,196
Yale (Colorado)	4,327	14,196
Elgon (volcanic) (Uganda-Kenya)	4,322	14,178
Shasta (volcanic) (California)	4,317	14,162
Grand Combin (Switzerland)	4,314	14,153
San Luis (Colorado)	4,312	14,146
Batu (Ethiopia)	4,307	14,130
Pikes Peak (Colorado)	4,301	14,110
Snowmass (Colorado)	4,291	14,077
Culebra (Colorado)	4,286	14,070

Name (location)	Height (m)	Height (ft)
Sunlight (Colorado)	4,284	14,053
Split (California)	4,283	14,051
Redcloud (Colorado)	4,278	14,034
Finsteraarhorn (Switzerland)	4,274	14,022
Wrangell (Alaska)	4,269	14,005
Mount of the Holy Cross (Colorado)	4,266	13,996
Humphreys (California)	4,259	13,972
Ouray (Colorado)	4,254	13,955
Guna (Ethiopia)	4,231	13,881
Mauna Kea (Hawaii)	4,207	13,800

Name	Height	Height
(location)	*(m)*	*(ft)*
Gannet		
(Wyoming)	4,202	13,785
Hayes		
(Alaska)	4,188	13,740
Fremont		
(Wyoming)	4,185	13,730
Sidley		
(Antarctica)	4,181	13,717
Mauna Loa (volcanic)		
(Hawii)	4,170	13,680
Jungfrau		
(Switzerland)	4,159	13,642
Kings		
(Utah)	4,124	13,528
Kinabalu		
(Sabah)	4,102	13,455
Cameroon (volcanic)		
(Cameroun)	4,070	13,352
Fridtjof Nansen		
(Antarctica)	4,068	13,346

Name (location)	Height (m)	Height (ft)
Tacaná (volcanic) (Mexico-Guatemala)	4,064	13,333
Bernina (Switzerland)	4,049	13,284
Summit (Colorado)	4,046	13,272
Waddington (British Colombia, Canada)	4,042	13,260
Lister (Antarctica)	4,025	13,205
Cloud Peak (Wyoming)	4,016	13,176
Yu Shan (Taiwan)	3,997	13,113
Truchas (New Mexico)	3,994	13,102
Wheeler (Nevada)	3,981	13,058
Robson (British Colmbia, Canada)	3,954	12,972

Name (location)	Height (m)	Height (ft)
Granite (Montana)	3,902	12,799
Borah (Idaho)	3,858	12,655
Baldy (New Mexico)	3,848	12,623
Monte Viso (Italy)	3,847	12,621
Kerinci (volcanic) (Sumatra)	3,805	12,483
Grossglockner (Austria)	3,798	12,460
Erebus (volcanic) (Antarctica)	3,794	12,447
Excelsior (California)	3,790	12,434
Fujiyama (volcanic) (Japan)	3,776	12,388
Cook (New Zealand)	3,764	12,349

Name *(location)*	Height *(m)*	Height *(ft)*
Adams (Washington)	3,752	12,307
Lanín (volcanic) (Argentina-Chile)	3,740	12,270
Teyde or Tenerife (volcanic) (Canary Islands)	3,718	12,198
Mahameru (volcanic) (Java)	3,676	12,060
Assiniboine (British Colombia-Alberta, Canada)	3,618	11,870
Hood (vocanic) (Oregon)	3,428	11,245
Pico de Aneto (Spain)	3,404	11,168
Rheinwaldhorn (Switzerland)	3,402	11,161
Perdido (Spain)	3,352	10,997
Etna (volcanic) (Sicily)	3,323	10,902

Name (location)	Height (m)	Height (ft)
Baker (Washington)	3,286	10,778
Lassen (volcanic) (California)	3,188	10,457
Dempo (volcanic) (Sumatra)	3,159	10,364
Siple (Antarctica)	3,100	10,170
Montcalm (France)	3,080	10,105
Haleakala (volcanic) (Hawaii)	3,058	10,032
St. Helens (Washington)	2,950	9,677
Pulog (Philippines)	2,934	9,626
Tahat (Algeria)	2,918	9,573
Shishaldin (volcanic) (Aleutian Islands)	2,862	9,387

Name (location)	Height (m)	Height (ft)
Roraima (Brazil-Venezuela-Guyana)	2,810	9,219
Ruapehu (volcanic) (New Zealand)	2,797	9,175
Katherine (Egypt)	2,637	8,651
Doi Inthanon (Thailand)	2,594	8,510
Galdhöpiggen (Norway)	2,469	8,100
Parnassus (Greece)	2,457	8,061
Olympus (Washington)	2,425	7,954
Kosciusko (Australia)	2,230	7,316
Harney (South Dakota)	2,208	7,242
Mitchell (North Carolina)	2,038	6,684

Name (location)	Height (m)	Height (ft)
Clingmans Dome (North Carolina-Tennessee)	2,025	6,642
Washington (New Hampshire)	1,917	6,288
Rogers (Virginia)	1,807	5,927
Marcy (New York)	1,629	5,344
Cirque (Labrador)	1,573	5,160
Pelée (volcanic) (Martinique)	1,463	4,800
Ben Nevis (Scotland)	1,343	4,406
Vesuvius (volcanic) (Italy)	1,278	4,190

Principal Rivers of The World

Name (location)	Length (m)	Length (ft)
Nile (Africa)	6,695	4,160
Amazon (South America)	6,518	4,050
Yangtze (Chang Jiang) (Asia)	6,381	3,965
(Mississippi-Missouri) (North America)	6,019	3,740
Ob-Irtysh (Asia)	5,569	3,460
Yenisel-Angara (Asia)	5,553	3,450
Hwang Ho (Huang He) (Asia)	5,464	3,395
Zaire (Africa)	4,668	2,900
Mekong (Asia)	4,426	2,750

Name (location)	Length (m)	Length (ft)
Amur (Asia)	4,416	2,744
Lena (Asia)	4,394	2,730
Mackenzie (North America)	4,249	2,640
Niger (Africa)	4,032	2,505
Paraná (South America)	4,000	2,485
Missouri (North America)	3,969	2,466
Mississippi (North America)	3,779	2,348
Murray-Darling (Australia)	3,750	2,330
Volga (Europe)	3,686	2,290
Darling (Australia)	3,203	1,990

Name (location)	Length (m)	Length (ft)
Madeira (South America)	3,203	1,990
St. Lawrence (North America)	3,203	1,990
Yukon (North America)	3,187	1,980
Indus (Asia)	3,179	1,975
Syr Darya (Asia)	3,079	1,913
Salween (Asia)	3,060	1,901
Rio Grande (North America)	3,034	1,885
São Francisco (South America)	2,897	1,800
Danube (Europe)	2,849	1,770
Brahmaputra (Asia)	2,841	1,765

Name (location)	Length (m)	Length (ft)
Euphrates (Asia)	2,817	1,750
Pará-Tocantins (South America)	2,752	1,710
Zambezi (Africa)	2,656	1,650
Amu Darya (Asia)	2,624	1,630
Paraguay (South America)	2,600	1,615
Nelson-Saskatchewan (North America)	2,575	1,600
Ural (Asia)	2,535	1,575
Kolyma (Asia)	2,514	1,562
Ganges (Asia)	2,511	1,560
Orinoco (South America)	2,503	1,555

Name (location)	Length (m)	Length (ft)
Arkansas (North America)	2,350	1,460
Colorado (North America)	2,334	1,450
Dnepr (Europe)	2,286	1,420
Negro (South America)	2,254	1,400
Aldan (Asia)	2,242	1,393
Irrawaddy (Asia)	2,149	1,335
Xi Jiang (Asia)	2,130	1,323
Ohio (North America)	2,102	1,306
Orange (Africa)	2,093	1,300
Kama (Europe)	2,028	1,260

Name (location)	Length (m)	Length (ft)
Xingú (South America)	2,012	1,250
Columbia (North America)	1,954	1,214
Juruá (South America)	1,932	1,200
Tigris (Asia)	1,899	1,180
Don (Europe)	1,871	1,162
Pechora (Europe)	1,814	1,127
Araguaya (South America)	1,771	1,100
Peace (North America)	1,714	1,065
Snake (North America)	1,671	1,038
Red (North America)	1,639	1,018

Name (location)	Length (m)	Length (ft)
Churchill (North America)	1,610	1,000
Marañón (South America)	1,610	1,000
Pilcomayo (South America)	1,610	1,000
Ucayali (South America)	1,610	1,000
Uruguay (South America)	1,610	1,000
Magdalena (South America)	1,529	950
Oka (Europe)	1,481	920
Canadian (North America)	1,459	906
Godavari (Asia)	1,449	900
Parnaíba (South America)	1,449	900

Name (location)	Length (m)	Length (ft)
Dnestr (Europe)	1,412	877
Brazos (North America)	1,401	870
Fraser (North America)	1,368	850
Salado (South America)	1,368	850
Rhine (Europe)	1,320	820
Narmada (Asia)	1,288	800
Tobol (Asia)	1,288	800
Athabaska (North America)	1,232	765
Pecos (North America)	1,183	735
Green (North America)	1,175	730

Name (location)	Length (m)	Length (ft)
Elbe (Europe)	1,167	725
Ottawa (North America)	1,121	696
White (North America)	1,111	690
Cumberland (North America)	1,106	687
Yellowstone (North America)	1,080	671
Donets (Europe)	1,079	670
Tennesse (North America)	1,050	652
Vistula (Europe)	1,014	630
Loire (Europe)	1,013	629
Tagus (Europe)	1,006	625

Name (location)	Length (m)	Length (ft)
Tisza (Europe)	997	619
North Platte (North America)	995	618
Ouachita (North America)	974	605
Sava (Europe)	940	584
Neman (Europe)	937	582
Oder (Europe)	910	565
Cimarron (North America)	805	c.500
Gila (North America)	805	c.500
Gambia (Africa)	483	300

Principal Lakes of The World

Name	Location	Area (sq km)	Area (sq mi)	Length (km)	Length (mi)	Max. Depth (m)	(ft)
Caspian	Asia-Europe	370,899	143,205	1,172	728	980	3,215
Superior	North America	83,242	32,140	564	350	393	1,289
Victoria	Africa	68,790	26,560	363	225	100	328
Aral	Asia	65,488	25,285	379	235	68	223
Michigan	North America	58,003	22,395	495	307	281	922
Tanganyika	Africa	32,893	12,700	676	420	1,435	4,708
Great Bear	North America	31,779	12,270	309	192	319	1,047
Baikal	Asia	30,498	11,775	636	395	1,741	5,712

Name	Location	Area (sq km)	Area (sq mi)	Length (km)	Length (mi)	Max. Depth (m)	(ft)
Nyasa	Africa	28,879	11,150	580	360	706	2,316
Great Slave	North America	28,439	10,980	480	298	140	459
Erie	North America	25,680	9,915	388	241	64	210
Winnipeg	North America	24,502	9,460	429	266	21	69
Ontario	North America	19,231	7,425	311	193	237	778
Ladoga	Europe	18,389	7,100	200	124	230	755
Balkhash	Asia	17,392	6,715	605	376	26	85
Chad	Africa	10,360-25,900	4,000-10,000	210	130	4-7	13-23
Onega	Europe	9,596	3,705	234	145	124	407
Eyre	Australia	0-8,897	0-3,435	145	90	0-21	0-66

Titicaca	South America	8,288	3,200	197	122	304	997
Nicaragua	Central America	8,263	3,190	165	102	71	230
Athabaska	North America	8,081	3,120	335	208	92	299
Turkana	Africa	7,105	2,743	248	154	74	240
Reindeer	North America	6,398	2,470	250	155		
Issyk-Kul	Asia	6,204	2,395	186	115	702	2,303
Urmia	Asia	5,906	2,280	145	90	15	49
Torrens	Australia	5,776	2,230	210	130		
Vänern	Europe	5,582	2,155	147	91	99	322
Winnipegosis	North America	5,403	2,086	227	141	12	38
Albert	Africa	5,346	2,064	161	100	52	168
Mweru	Africa	4,921	1,900	73	45	14	46
Nipigon	North America	4,844	1,870	116	72	165	540

Name	Location	Area (sq km)	Area (sq mi)	Length (km)	Length (mi)	Max. Depth (m)	(ft)
Manitoba	North America	4,707	1,817	226	140		
Qinghai Hu	Asia	4,144	1,600	110	68	39	125
Lake of the Woods	North America	3,847	1,485	116	72	21	69
Van	Asia	3,712	1,433	129	80	25	82
Great Salt Lake	N America	2,590-5,180	1,000-2,000	121	75	11	35
Dead Sea	Asia	1,021	394	74	46		

The areas of some of these lakes are subject to seasonal variations.

Principal Waterfalls of The World

Name (location)	Height (m)	Height (ft)
Angel (Venezuela)	808	2,648
Yosemite (California) (including upper, central and lower falls, and rapids)	740	2,425
Kukenaām (Guyana)	610	2,000
Sutherland (New Zealand)	581	1,904
Wolloomombie (Australia)	519	1,700
Ribbon (California)	492	1,612
Upper Yosemite (California)	436	1,430
Gavarnie (France)	422	1,384

Name (location)	Height (m)	Height (ft)
Tugela (South Africa)	412	1,350
Takkakau (British Colombia)	366	1,200
Staubbach (Switzerland)	300	984
Trümmelbach (Switzerland)	290	950
Middle Cascade (California)	278	910
Vettisfoss (Norway)	271	889
King Edward VIII (Guyana)	256	840
Gersoppa (India)	253	830
Skykjefos (Norway)	250	820
Kajeteur (Guyana)	226	741

Name *(locatiõn)*	Height *(m)*	Height *(ft)*
Kalambo (Zambia)	222	726
Maradalsfos (Norway)	199	650
Maletsunyane (South Africa)	192	630
Bridalveil (California)	189	620
Multnomah (Oregon)	189	620
Vöringfoss (Norway)	182	597
Nevada (California)	181	594
Terni (Italy)	180	590
Skjeggedalsfoss (Norway)	160	525
Marina (Guyana)	153	500

Name (location)	Height (m)	Height (ft)
Aughrabies (South Africa)	147	480
Tequendama (Colombia)	131	427
Guaíra (Brazil-Paraguay)	114	374
Illilouette (California)	113	370
Victoria (Zambia and Zimbabwe)	109	355
Kegon-no-tali (Japan)	101	330
Lower Yosemite (California)	98	320
Cauvery (India)	98	320
Vernal (California)	97	317
Virginia (North West Territories	96	315

Name (location)	Height (m)	Height (ft)
Lower Yellowstone (Wyoming)	94	308
Churchill (Labrador)	92	302
Reichenbach (Switzerland)	91	300
Sluiskin (Washington)	91	300
Lower Gastein (Austria)	86	280
Paulo Alfonso (Brazil)	84	275
Snoqualmie (Washington)	82	268
Seven (Colorado)	81	266
Montmorency (Quebec)	77	251
Handegg (Switzerland)	76	250

Name (location)	Height (m)	Height (ft)
Taughannock (New York)	66	215
Iguassú (Brazil)	64	210
Shoshone (Idaho)	64	210
Upper Gastein (Austria)	63	207
Comet (Washington)	61	200
Narada (Washington)	52	168
Niagara (New York-Ontario)	51	167
Tower (Wyoming)	41	132
Stora Sjöfallet (Sweden)	40	131
Kabalega (Uganda)	40	130
Upper Yellowstone (Wyoming)	34	109

Distances between International Airports

Cities	km	miles
Athens — Bahrain	2 829	1 758
Athens — London	2 414	1 500
Athens — Paris	2 093	1 300
Athens — Rome	1 047	651
Bahrain — Bangkok	5 358	3 330
Bahrain — Hong Kong	6 389	3 970
Bahrain — London	5 090	3 163
Bahrain — New York	10 614	6 600
Bangkok — Bombay	3 008	1 869
Bangkok — London	9 540	5 928
Bangkok — Nairobi	7 207	4 478
Bangkok — Singapore	1 443	897

Cities	km	miles
Bombay — Buenos Aires	14 935	9 281
Bombay — London	7 207	4 478
Bombay — Nairobi	4 529	2 815
Bombay — Tokyo	6 782	4 215
Buenos Aires — Cairo	11 844	7 360
Buenos Aires — Frankfurt	11 494	7 142
Buenos Aires — London	11 129	6 916
Buenos Aires — Mexico City	7 391	4 593
Cairo — Chicago	9 866	6 131
Cairo — Lagos	3 927	2 441
Cairo — London	3 531	2 195
Cairo — Peking	7 530	4 679

Cities	km	miles
Chicago — Copenhagen	6 849	4 256
Chicago — London	6 343	3 942
Chicago — New York	1 187	738
Chicago — Rome	7 734	4 806
Copenhagen — Frankfurt	678	421
Copenhagen — London	982	611
Copenhagen — Rome	1 535	954
Copenhagen — Vancouver	7 657	4 758
Frankfurt — Hong Kong	9 165	5 695
Frankfurt — London	654	407
Frankfurt — Moscow	2 021	1 256
Frankfurt — Paris	471	293

Cities	km	miles
Hong Kong — Karachi	4 775	2 967
Hong Kong — London	9 640	5 990
Hong Kong — Peking	1 985	1 233
Hong Kong — Singapore	2 576	1 601
Karachi — London	6 334	3 936
Karachi — Nairobi	4 367	2 714
Karachi — Rio de Janeiro	13 004	8 081
Karachi — Tokyo	6 969	4 331
London — Madrid	1 244	773
London — Moscow	2 506	1 557
London — New York	5 536	3 440
London — Paris	365	227

Cities	km	miles
Madrid — Manila	11 644	7 236
Madrid — New York	5 758	3 578
Madrid — Paris	1 031	641
Madrid — Rome	1 359	845
Manila — London	10 758	6 685
Manila — Mexico City	14 218	8 835
Manila — Moscow	8 273	5 141
Manila — Sydney	6 258	3 889
Mexico City — London	8 899	5 530
Mexico City — Montreal	3 712	2 307
Mexico City — Rio de Janeiro	7 661	4 761
Mexico City — Singapore	16 587	10 307

Cities	km	miles
Montreal — London	5 213	3 240
Montreal — Moscow	7 036	4 372
Montreal — San Francisco	4 072	2 530
Montreal — Vancouver	3 679	2 286
Moscow — Nairobi	6 366	3 956
Moscow — Paris	2 479	1 541
Moscow — Sydney	6 313	3 923
Moscow — Tokyo	7 502	4 662
Nairobi — London	6 836	4 248
Nairobi — New York	11 828	7 351
Nairobi — Paris	6 475	4 024
Nairobi — Rome	5 380	3 343

Cities	km	miles
New York — Paris	5 829	3 622
New York — San Francisco	4 149	2 578
New York — Sydney	16 002	9 944
New York — Tokyo	10 824	6 726
Paris — Peking	8 214	5 104
Paris — Rome	1 100	684
Paris — Sydney	16 954	10 535
Paris — Tokyo	9 736	6 049
Peking — London	8 148	5 063
Peking — Rome	8 120	5 046
Peking — Singapore	4 486	2 788
Peking — Tokyo	2 133	1 326

Cities	km	miles
Rio de Janeiro — Rome	9 186	5 708
Rio de Janeiro — London	9 245	5 745
Rio de Janeiro — Buenos Aires	1 996	1 241
Rio de Janeiro — Vancouver	11 206	6 963
Rome — Athens	1 047	651
Rome — San Francisco	10 052	6 246
Rome — Singapore	10 010	6 220
Rome — London	1 460	907
San Francisco — London	8 610	5 350
San Francisco — Singapore	13 579	8 438
San Francisco — Sydney	11 941	7 420
San Francisco — Vancouver	1 286	799

Cities	km	miles
Singapore — London	10 873	6 757
Singapore — Sydney	6 290	3 908
Singapore — Tokyo	5 361	3 331
Singapore — Sydney	6 290	3 908
Sydney — Hong Kong	7 374	4 582
Sydney — Vancouver	12 492	7 763
Sydney — London	17 008	10 569
Sydney — Tokyo	7 826	4 863
Tokyo — Bangkok	4 642	2 885
Tokyo — Vancouver	7 500	4 660
Tokyo — London	9 585	5 956
Tokyo — San Francisco	8 222	5 109

WORLDWIDE
WEATHER
GUIDE

Accra

	J	F	M	A	M	J	J	A	S	O	N	D
Temperature °F Max	87	88	88	88	87	84	81	80	81	85	87	88
Min	73	75	76	76	75	74	73	71	73	74	75	75
Temperature °C Max	31	31	31	31	31	29	28	28	28	29	31	31
Min	23	24	24	24	24	23	23	22	23	23	24	24
Humidity % am	95	96	95	95	96	96	97	97	96	97	97	97
pm	61	61	63	65	68	64	76	77	72	71	66	64

Amsterdam

	J	F	M	A	M	J	J	A	S	O	N	D
Temperature °F Max	40	42	49	56	64	70	72	71	67	57	48	42
Min	31	31	34	40	46	51	55	55	50	44	38	33
Temperature °C Max	4	5	10	13	18	21	22	22	19	14	9	5
Min	-1	-1	1	4	8	11	13	13	10	7	3	1
Humidity % am	90	90	86	79	75	75	79	82	86	90	92	91
pm	82	76	65	61	59	59	64	65	67	72	81	85

Athens

	J	F	M	A	M	J	J	A	S	O	N	D
Temperature °F Max	55	57	60	68	77	86	92	92	84	85	66	58
Min	44	44	46	52	61	68	73	73	67	60	53	47
Temperature °C Max	13	14	16	20	25	30	33	33	29	24	19	15
Min	6	7	8	11	16	20	23	23	19	15	12	8
Humidity % am	77	74	71	65	60	50	47	48	58	70	78	78
pm	62	57	54	48	47	39	34	34	42	52	61	63

Auckland

	J	F	M	A	M	J	J	A	S	O	N	D
Temperature °F Max	73	73	71	67	62	58	56	58	60	63	66	70
Min	60	60	59	56	51	48	46	46	49	52	54	57
Temperature °C Max	23	23	22	19	17	14	13	14	16	17	19	21
Min	16	16	15	13	11	9	8	8	9	11	12	14
Humidity % am	71	72	74	78	80	83	84	80	76	74	71	70
pm	62	61	65	69	70	73	74	70	68	66	64	64

Bahrain

	J	F	M	A	M	J	J	A	S	O	N	D
Temperature °F Max	68	70	75	84	92	96	99	100	96	90	82	71
Min	57	59	63	70	78	82	85	85	81	75	69	60
Temperature °C Max	20	21	24	29	33	36	37	38	36	32	28	22
Min	14	15	17	21	26	28	29	29	27	24	21	16
Humidity % am	85	83	80	75	71	69	74	75	75	80	80	85
pm	71	70	70	66	63	64	67	65	64	66	70	77

Bangkok

	J	F	M	A	M	J	J	A	S	O	N	D
Temperature °F Max	89	91	93	95	93	91	90	90	89	88	87	87
Min	68	72	75	77	77	76	76	76	76	75	72	68
Temperature °C Max	32	33	34	35	34	33	32	32	32	31	31	31
Min	20	22	24	25	25	24	24	24	24	25	22	20
Humidity % am	91	92	92	90	91	90	91	92	94	93	92	91
pm	53	55	56	58	64	67	66	66	70	70	65	56

Beirut

		J	F	M	A	M	J	J	A	S	O	N	D
Temperature°F	Max	62	63	66	72	78	83	87	89	86	81	73	65
	Min	51	51	54	58	64	69	73	74	73	69	61	55
Temperature°C	Max	17	17	19	22	26	28	31	32	30	27	23	18
	Min	11	11	12	14	18	21	23	23	23	21	16	12
Humidity %	am	72	72	72	72	69	67	66	65	64	65	67	70
	pm	70	70	69	67	64	61	58	57	57	62	61	69

Berlin

		J	F	M	A	M	J	J	A	S	O	N	D
Temperature°F	Max	35	37	46	56	66	72	75	74	68	56	45	38
	Min	26	26	31	39	47	53	57	56	50	42	36	29
Temperature°C	Max	2	3	8	13	19	22	24	23	20	13	7	3
	Min	-3	-3	0	4	8	12	14	13	10	6	2	-1
Humidity %	am	89	89	88	84	80	84	88	92	92	93	92	91
	pm	82	78	67	60	57	58	61	61	65	73	83	86

Bombay

	J	F	M	A	M	J	J	A	S	O	N	D
Temperature °F Max	83	83	86	89	91	89	85	85	85	89	89	97
Min	67	67	72	76	80	79	77	76	76	76	73	79
Temperature °C Max	28	28	30	32	33	32	29	29	29	32	32	31
Min	12	12	17	20	23	21	22	22	22	21	18	13
Humidity % am	70	71	73	75	74	79	83	83	85	81	73	70
pm	61	62	65	67	68	77	83	81	78	71	64	62

Brussels

	J	F	M	A	M	J	J	A	S	O	N	D
Temperature °F Max	40	44	51	58	65	72	73	72	69	60	48	42
Min	30	32	36	41	46	52	54	54	51	45	38	32
Temperature °C Max	4	7	10	14	18	22	23	22	21	15	9	6
Min	-1	0	2	5	8	11	12	12	11	7	3	0
Humidity % am	92	92	91	91	90	87	91	93	94	93	93	92
pm	86	81	74	71	65	65	68	69	69	77	85	86

Buenos Aires

	J	F	M	A	M	J	J	A	S	O	N	D
Temperature °F Max	85	83	79	72	64	57	57	60	64	69	76	82
Min	63	63	60	53	47	41	42	43	46	50	56	61
Temperature °C Max	29	28	26	22	18	14	14	16	18	21	24	28
Min	17	17	16	12	8	5	6	6	8	10	13	16
Humidity % am	81	83	87	88	90	91	92	90	86	83	79	79
pm	61	63	69	71	74	78	79	74	68	65	60	62

Cairo

	J	F	M	A	M	J	J	A	S	O	N	D
Temperature °F Max	65	69	75	83	91	95	96	95	90	86	78	68
Min	47	48	52	57	63	68	70	71	68	65	58	50
Temperature °C Max	18	21	24	28	33	35	36	35	32	30	26	20
Min	8	9	11	14	17	20	20	22	20	18	14	10
Humidity % am	69	64	63	55	50	55	65	69	68	67	68	70
pm	40	33	27	21	18	20	24	28	31	31	38	41

	J	F	M	A	M	J	J	A	S	O	N	D
Calcutta												
Temperature °F Max	80	84	93	97	96	92	89	89	90	89	84	79
Min	55	59	69	75	77	79	79	78	78	74	64	55
Temperature °C Max	27	29	34	36	36	33	32	32	32	32	29	26
Min	13	15	21	24	25	26	26	26	26	24	18	13
Humidity % am	85	82	79	76	77	82	86	88	86	85	79	80
pm	52	45	46	56	62	75	80	82	81	72	63	55
Christchurch												
Temperature °F Max	70	69	66	62	56	51	50	52	57	62	66	69
Min	53	53	50	45	40	36	35	36	40	44	47	51
Temperature °C Max	21	21	19	17	13	11	10	11	14	17	19	21
Min	12	12	10	7	4	2	2	2	4	7	8	11
Humidity % am	65	71	75	82	85	97	97	81	72	63	64	67
pm	59	60	69	71	69	72	76	66	69	60	64	60

Colombo

	J	F	M	A	M	J	J	A	S	O	N	D
Temperature °F Max	86	87	88	88	87	85	85	85	85	85	85	85
Min	72	72	74	76	78	77	77	77	77	75	73	72
Temperature °C Min	30	31	31	31	31	29	29	29	29	29	29	29
Min	22	22	23	24	25	26	25	25	25	24	23	22
Humidity % am	73	71	71	74	78	80	79	78	78	77	77	74
pm	67	66	66	70	76	78	77	77	76	76	75	69

Copenhagen

	J	F	M	A	M	J	J	A	S	O	N	D
Temperature °F Max	36	36	41	51	61	67	71	70	64	54	45	40
Min	28	28	31	38	46	52	57	56	51	44	38	34
Temperature °C Max	2	2	5	10	16	19	22	21	18	12	7	4
Min	-2	-3	-1	3	8	11	14	14	11	7	3	1
Humidity % am	88	86	85	79	70	70	74	78	83	86	88	89
pm	85	83	78	68	59	60	62	64	69	76	83	87

Delhi

		J	F	M	A	M	J	J	A	S	O	N	D
Temperature °F	Max	70	75	87	97	105	102	96	93	93	93	84	73
	Min	44	49	58	68	79	83	81	79	75	65	52	46
Temperature °C	Max	21	24	31	36	41	39	36	34	34	34	29	23
	Min	7	9	14	20	26	28	27	26	24	18	11	8
Humidity %	am	72	67	49	35	35	53	75	80	72	56	51	69
	pm	41	35	23	19	20	36	59	64	51	32	31	42

Djakarta

		J	F	M	A	M	J	J	A	S	O	N	D
Temperature °F	Max	84	84	86	87	87	87	87	87	88	87	86	85
	Min	74	74	74	75	75	74	73	73	74	74	74	74
Temperature °C	Max	29	29	30	31	31	31	31	31	31	31	30	29
	Min	23	23	23	24	24	23	23	23	23	23	23	23
Humidity %	am	95	95	94	94	94	93	92	90	90	90	92	92
	pm	75	75	73	71	69	67	64	61	62	64	68	71

	J	F	M	A	M	J	J	A	S	O	N	D
Frankfurt												
Temperature °F Max	38	41	51	60	69	74	77	76	69	58	47	39
Min	29	30	35	42	49	55	58	57	52	44	38	32
Temperature °C Max	3	5	11	16	20	23	25	24	21	14	8	4
Min	-1	-2	2	6	9	13	15	14	11	7	3	0
Humidity % am	86	86	84	79	78	78	81	85	89	91	89	88
pm	77	70	57	51	50	52	53	54	60	68	77	81
Haifa												
Temperature °F Max	65	67	71	77	83	85	88	90	88	85	78	68
Min	49	50	53	58	65	71	75	76	74	68	60	53
Temperature °C Max	18	19	22	25	28	29	31	32	31	29	26	20
Min	9	10	12	14	18	22	24	24	23	20	16	12
Humidity % am	66	65	62	60	62	67	70	70	67	66	61	66
pm	56	56	56	57	59	66	68	69	66	66	56	56

Hamilton, Bda.

	J	F	M	A	M	J	J	A	S	O	N	D
Temperature °F Max	68	68	68	71	76	81	85	86	84	79	74	70
Min	58	57	57	59	64	69	73	74	72	69	63	60
Temperature °C Max	20	20	20	22	24	27	29	30	29	26	23	21
Min	14	14	14	15	18	21	23	23	22	21	17	16
Humidity % am	78	78	77	78	81	82	81	79	81	79	76	77
pm	70	69	69	70	75	74	73	69	73	72	70	70

Harare

	J	F	M	A	M	J	J	A	S	O	N	D
Temperature °F Max	78	78	78	78	74	70	70	74	79	83	81	79
Min	60	60	58	55	49	44	44	47	53	58	60	60
Temperature °C Max	26	26	26	26	23	21	21	23	26	28	27	26
Min	16	16	14	13	9	7	7	8	12	14	16	16
Humidity % am	74	77	75	68	60	58	56	50	43	43	56	67
pm	57	53	52	44	37	36	33	28	26	26	43	57

Hong Kong

	J	F	M	A	M	J	J	A	S	O	N	D
Temperature °F Max	64	63	67	75	82	85	87	87	85	81	74	68
Min	56	55	60	67	74	78	78	78	77	73	65	59
Temperature °C Max	18	17	19	24	28	29	31	31	29	27	23	20
Min	13	13	16	19	23	26	26	26	25	23	18	15
Humidity % am	77	82	84	87	87	86	87	87	83	75	73	74
pm	66	73	74	77	78	77	77	77	72	63	60	63

Instanbul

	J	F	M	A	M	J	J	A	S	O	N	D
Temperature °F Max	46	47	51	60	69	77	82	82	76	68	59	51
Min	37	36	38	45	53	60	65	66	61	55	48	41
Temperature °C Max	8	8	11	16	21	25	28	28	24	20	15	11
Min	3	2	3	7	12	16	18	19	16	13	9	5
Humidity % am	82	82	81	81	82	79	79	79	81	83	82	82
pm	75	72	67	62	61	58	56	55	59	64	71	74

Jeddah

	J	F	M	A	M	J	J	A	S	O	N	D
Temperature °F Max	84	84	85	91	95	97	99	99	96	95	91	88
Min	66	65	67	70	74	75	79	80	87	83	81	67
Temperature °C Max	29	29	29	33	35	36	37	37	36	35	33	30
Min	19	18	19	21	23	24	26	27	25	23	22	19
Humidity % am	58	52	52	52	51	56	55	59	65	60	55	55
pm	54	52	52	56	55	55	50	51	61	61	59	54

Johannesburg

	J	F	M	A	M	J	J	A	S	O	N	D
Temperature °F Max	78	77	75	72	66	62	63	68	73	77	77	78
Min	58	58	55	50	43	39	39	43	48	53	55	57
Temperature °C Max	26	25	24	22	19	17	17	20	23	25	25	26
Min	14	14	13	10	6	4	4	6	9	12	13	14
Humidity % am	75	78	79	74	70	70	69	64	59	64	67	70
pm	50	53	50	44	36	33	32	29	30	37	45	47

Kathmandu

	J	F	M	A	M	J	J	A	S	O	N	D
Temperature °F Max	65	67	77	83	86	85	84	83	83	80	74	67
Min	35	39	45	53	61	67	68	68	66	56	45	37
Temperature °C Max	18	19	25	28	30	29	29	28	28	27	23	19
Min	2	4	7	12	16	19	20	20	19	13	7	3
Humidity % am	89	90	73	68	72	79	86	87	86	88	90	89
pm	70	68	53	54	61	72	82	84	83	81	78	73

Kuala Lumpur

	J	F	M	A	M	J	J	A	S	O	N	D
Temperature °F Max	90	92	92	91	91	90	90	90	89	89	89	89
Min	72	72	73	74	73	72	73	73	73	73	73	72
Temperature °C Max	32	33	33	33	33	32	32	32	32	32	32	32
Min	22	22	23	23	23	22	23	23	23	23	23	22
Humidity % am	97	97	97	97	97	95	96	96	96	96	97	97
pm	60	60	58	63	66	63	62	64	65	66	66	61

Lagos

		J	F	M	A	M	J	J	A	S	O	N	D
Temperature °F	Max	88	89	89	89	87	85	83	82	83	85	88	88
	Min	74	77	78	77	76	74	74	73	74	74	75	75
Temperature °C	Max	31	32	32	32	31	29	28	28	28	29	31	31
	Min	23	25	26	25	24	23	23	23	23	23	24	24
Humidity %	am	84	83	82	81	83	87	87	85	86	86	85	86
	pm	65	69	72	72	76	80	80	76	77	76	72	68

Lima

		J	F	M	A	M	J	J	A	S	O	N	D
Temperature °F	Max	82	83	83	80	74	68	67	66	68	71	74	78
	Min	66	67	66	63	60	58	57	56	57	58	60	62
Temperature °C	Max	28	28	28	27	23	20	19	19	20	22	23	26
	Min	19	19	19	17	16	14	14	13	14	14	16	17
Humidity %	am	93	92	92	93	95	95	94	95	94	94	93	93
	pm	69	66	64	66	76	80	77	78	76	72	71	70

Lisbon

		J	F	M	A	M	J	J	A	S	O	N	D
Temperature °F	Max	57	59	63	67	71	77	81	82	79	72	63	58
	Min	46	47	50	53	55	60	63	63	62	58	52	47
Temperature °C	Max	14	15	17	20	21	25	27	28	26	22	17	15
	Min	8	8	10	12	13	15	17	17	17	14	11	9
Humidity %	am	85	80	78	69	68	65	62	64	70	75	81	84
	pm	71	64	64	56	57	54	48	49	54	59	68	72

London (UK)

		J	F	M	A	M	J	J	A	S	O	N	D
Temperature °F	Max	43	44	50	56	62	69	71	71	65	58	50	45
	Min	36	36	38	42	47	53	56	56	52	46	42	38
Temperature °C	Max	6	7	10	13	17	20	22	21	19	14	10	7
	Min	2	2	3	6	8	12	14	13	11	8	5	4
Humidiy %	am	86	85	81	71	70	70	71	76	80	85	85	87
	pm	77	72	64	56	57	58	59	62	65	70	78	81

	J	F	M	A	M	J	J	A	S	O	N	D
Madrid												
Temperature °F Max	47	52	59	65	70	80	87	85	77	65	55	48
Min	35	36	41	45	50	58	63	63	57	48	42	36
Temperature °C Max	9	11	15	18	21	27	31	30	25	19	13	9
Min	2	2	5	7	10	15	17	17	14	10	5	2
Humidity % am	86	83	80	74	72	66	58	62	72	81	84	86
pm	71	62	56	49	49	41	33	35	46	58	65	70
Manila												
Temperature °F Max	86	88	91	93	93	91	88	87	88	88	87	86
Min	69	69	71	73	75	75	75	75	75	74	72	70
Temperature °C Max	30	31	33	34	34	33	31	31	31	31	31	30
Min	21	21	22	23	24	24	24	24	24	23	22	21
Humidity % am	89	88	85	85	88	91	91	92	93	92	91	90
pm	63	59	55	55	61	68	74	73	73	71	69	67

Melbourne

		J	F	M	A	M	J	J	A	S	O	N	D
Temperature °F	Max	78	78	75	68	62	57	56	59	63	67	71	75
	Min	57	57	55	51	47	44	42	43	46	48	51	54
Temperature °C	Max	26	26	24	20	17	14	13	15	17	19	22	24
	Min	14	14	13	11	8	7	6	6	8	9	11	12
Humidity %	am	58	62	64	72	79	83	82	76	68	61	60	59
	pm	48	50	51	56	62	67	65	60	55	52	52	51

Mexico City

		J	F	M	A	M	J	J	A	S	O	N	D
Temperature °F	Max	66	69	75	77	78	76	73	73	74	70	68	66
	Min	42	43	47	51	54	55	53	54	53	50	46	43
Temperature °C	Max	19	21	24	25	26	24	23	23	23	21	20	19
	Min	6	6	8	11	12	13	12	12	12	10	8	6
Humidity %	am	79	72	68	66	69	82	84	85	86	83	82	81
	pm	34	28	26	29	29	48	50	50	54	47	41	37

Miami

	J	F	M	A	M	J	J	A	S	O	N	D
Temperature °F Max	74	75	78	80	84	86	88	88	87	83	78	76
Min	61	61	64	67	71	74	76	76	75	72	66	62
Temperature °C Max	23	24	26	27	29	30	31	31	31	28	26	24
Min	16	16	18	19	22	22	24	24	24	22	19	17
Humidity % am	81	82	77	73	75	75	75	76	79	80	77	82
pm	66	63	62	64	67	69	68	68	70	69	64	65

Moscow

	J	F	M	A	M	J	J	A	S	O	N	D
Temperature °F Max	15	22	32	50	66	70	73	72	61	48	35	24
Min	3	8	18	34	46	51	55	53	45	37	26	15
Temperature °C Max	-9	-6	0	10	19	21	23	22	16	9	2	-5
Min	-16	-14	-8	1	8	11	13	12	7	3	-3	-10
Humidity % am	82	82	82	73	58	62	68	74	78	81	87	85
pm	77	66	64	54	43	47	54	55	59	67	79	83

Nairobi

		J	F	M	A	M	J	J	A	S	O	N	D
Temperature °F	Max	77	79	77	75	72	70	69	70	75	76	74	74
	Min	54	55	57	58	56	53	51	52	52	55	56	55
Temperature °C	Max	25	26	25	24	22	21	21	21	24	24	23	23
	Min	12	13	14	14	13	12	11	11	11	13	13	13
Humidity %	am	74	74	81	88	88	89	86	86	82	82	86	81
	pm	44	40	45	56	62	60	58	56	45	43	53	53

Nassau

		J	F	M	A	M	J	J	A	S	O	N	D
Temperature °F	Max	77	77	79	81	84	87	88	89	88	85	81	79
	Min	65	64	66	69	71	74	75	76	75	73	70	67
Temperature °C	Max	25	25	26	27	29	31	31	32	31	29	27	26
	Min	18	18	19	21	22	23	24	24	24	23	21	19
Humidity %	am	84	82	81	79	79	81	80	82	84	83	83	84
	pm	64	62	64	65	65	68	69	70	73	71	68	66

New York

		J	F	M	A	M	J	J	A	S	O	N	D
Temperature °F	Max	37	38	45	57	68	77	82	80	79	69	51	41
	Min	24	24	30	42	53	60	66	66	60	49	37	29
Temperature °C	Max	3	3	7	14	20	25	28	27	26	21	11	5
	Min	-4	-4	-1	6	12	16	19	19	16	9	3	-2
Humidity %	am	72	70	70	68	70	74	77	79	79	76	75	73
	pm	60	58	55	53	54	58	58	60	61	57	60	61

Oslo

		J	F	M	A	M	J	J	A	S	O	N	D
Temperature °F	Max	28	30	39	50	61	68	72	70	60	48	38	32
	Min	19	19	25	34	43	50	55	53	46	38	31	25
Temperature °C	Max	-2	-1	4	10	16	20	22	21	16	9	3	0
	Min	-7	-7	-4	1	6	10	13	12	8	3	-1	-4
Humidity %	am	86	84	80	75	68	69	74	79	85	88	88	87
	pm	82	74	64	57	52	55	59	61	66	72	83	85

Ottowa

	J	F	M	A	M	J	J	A	S	O	N	D
Temperature °F Max	21	22	33	51	66	76	81	77	68	54	39	24
Min	3	3	16	21	44	54	58	55	48	37	26	9
Temperature °C Max	-6	-6	1	11	19	24	27	25	20	12	4	-4
Min	-16	-16	-9	-1	7	12	14	13	9	3	-3	-13
Humidity % am	83	88	84	76	77	80	80	84	90	86	84	83
pm	76	73	66	58	55	56	53	54	59	63	68	75

Papeete

	J	F	M	A	M	J	J	A	S	O	N	D
Temperature °F Max	89	89	89	89	87	86	86	86	86	87	88	88
Min	72	72	72	72	70	69	68	68	69	70	71	72
Temperature °C Max	32	32	32	32	31	30	30	30	30	31	31	31
Min	22	22	22	22	21	21	20	20	21	21	22	22
Humidity % am	82	82	84	85	84	85	83	83	81	69	80	81
pm	77	77	78	78	78	79	77	78	76	76	77	78

Paris

	J	F	M	A	M	J	J	A	S	O	N	D
Temperature °F Max	42	45	55	61	69	75	80	79	73	61	50	43
Min	30	31	37	42	49	55	59	58	53	45	38	33
Temperature °C Max	5	7	13	16	20	24	27	26	23	16	10	6
Min	-1	0	3	6	9	13	15	14	12	7	4	0
Humidity % am	89	87	87	84	83	82	79	85	89	92	91	90
pm	80	72	60	56	56	55	50	54	60	69	78	80

Port-of-Spain

	J	F	M	A	M	J	J	A	S	O	N	D
Temperature °F Max	87	88	89	90	89	88	88	88	89	89	89	88
Min	69	68	68	69	71	71	71	71	71	71	71	69
Temperature °C Max	31	31	32	32	32	31	31	31	32	32	32	31
Min	21	20	20	21	22	22	22	22	22	22	22	21
Humidity % am	89	87	85	83	84	87	88	87	87	87	89	89
pm	68	65	63	61	63	69	71	73	74	74	76	71

Prague

		J	F	M	A	M	J	J	A	S	O	N	D
Temperature °F	Max	49	53	64	73	82	88	91	89	84	71	57	50
	Min	7	10	18	29	36	44	49	47	38	29	24	14
Temperature °C	Max	10	11	18	23	28	31	33	32	29	22	14	10
	Min	-13	-12	-8	-2	2	7	9	8	4	-2	-5	-10
Humidity %	am	84	83	82	77	75	74	77	81	84	87	87	87
	pm	73	67	55	47	45	46	49	48	51	60	73	78

Rangoon

		J	F	M	A	M	J	J	A	S	O	N	D
Temperature °F	Max	89	92	96	97	92	86	85	86	86	88	88	88
	Min	65	67	71	76	77	76	76	76	76	76	73	67
Temperature °C	Max	32	33	36	36	33	30	29	29	30	31	31	31
	Min	18	19	22	24	25	24	24	24	24	24	23	19
Humidity %	am	71	72	74	71	80	87	89	89	87	83	79	75
	pm	52	52	54	64	76	75	88	88	86	77	72	61

Rio de Janeiro

		J	F	M	A	M	J	J	A	S	O	N	D
Temperature °F	Max	84	85	83	80	77	76	75	76	75	77	79	82
	Min	73	73	72	69	66	64	63	64	65	66	68	71
Temperature °C	Max	29	29	28	27	25	24	24	24	24	25	26	28
	Min	23	23	22	21	19	18	17	18	18	19	20	22
Humidity %	am	82	84	87	87	87	87	86	84	84	83	82	82
	pm	70	71	74	73	70	69	68	66	72	72	72	72

Rome

		J	F	M	A	M	J	J	A	S	O	N	D
Temperature °F	Max	52	55	59	66	74	82	87	86	79	71	62	55
	Min	40	42	45	50	56	63	67	67	62	55	49	44
Temperature °C	Max	11	13	15	19	23	28	30	30	26	22	16	13
	Min	5	5	7	10	13	17	20	20	17	13	9	6
Humidity %	am	85	86	83	83	77	74	70	73	83	86	87	85
	pm	68	64	56	54	54	48	42	43	50	59	66	70

San Francisco

		J	F	M	A	M	J	J	A	S	O	N	D
Temperature °F	Max	55	59	61	62	63	66	65	65	69	68	63	57
	Min	45	47	48	49	51	52	53	53	55	54	51	47
Temperature °C	Max	13	15	16	17	17	18	19	18	21	20	17	14
	Min	7	8	9	9	11	11	12	12	13	12	11	8
Humidity %	am	85	84	83	83	85	88	91	92	88	85	83	83
	pm	69	66	61	61	62	64	69	70	60	58	60	68

Singapore

		J	F	M	A	M	J	J	A	S	O	N	D
Temperature °F	Max	86	88	88	88	89	88	88	87	87	87	87	87
	Min	73	73	75	75	75	75	75	75	75	74	74	74
Temperature °C	Max	30	31	31	31	34	31	31	31	31	31	31	31
	Min	23	23	24	24	24	24	24	24	24	23	23	23
Humidity %	am	82	77	76	77	79	79	79	78	79	78	79	82
	pm	78	71	70	74	73	73	72	72	72	72	75	78

	J	F	M	A	M	J	J	A	S	O	N	D
Stockholm												
Temperature °F Max	30	30	37	47	58	67	71	68	60	49	40	35
Min	23	22	26	34	43	51	57	56	49	41	34	29
Temperature °C Max	-1	-1	3	8	14	19	22	20	15	9	5	2
Min	-5	-5	-4	1	6	11	14	13	9	5	1	-2
Humidity % am	85	83	82	76	66	68	74	81	87	88	89	88
pm	83	77	68	60	53	55	59	64	69	76	85	86
Sydney												
Temperature °F Max	78	78	76	71	66	61	60	63	67	71	74	77
Min	65	65	63	58	52	48	46	48	51	56	60	63
Temperature °C Max	26	26	24	22	19	16	16	17	19	22	23	25
Min	18	18	17	14	11	9	8	9	11	13	16	17
Humidity % am	68	71	73	76	77	77	76	72	67	65	65	66
pm	64	65	65	64	63	62	60	56	55	57	60	62

Tehran

		J	F	M	A	M	J	J	A	S	O	N	D
Temperature °F	Max	45	50	59	71	82	93	99	97	90	76	63	51
	Min	27	32	39	49	58	66	72	71	64	53	43	33
Temperature °C	Max	7	10	15	22	28	34	37	36	32	24	17	11
	Min	-3	0	4	9	14	19	22	22	18	12	6	1
Humidity %	am	77	73	61	54	55	50	51	47	49	53	63	76
	pm	75	59	39	40	47	49	41	46	49	54	66	75

Tokyo

		J	F	M	A	M	J	J	A	S	O	N	D
Temperature °F	Max	47	48	54	63	71	76	83	86	79	69	60	52
	Min	29	31	36	46	54	63	70	72	66	55	43	33
Temperature °C	Max	8	9	12	17	22	24	28	30	26	21	16	11
	Min	-2	-1	2	8	12	17	21	22	19	13	6	1
Humidity %	am	73	71	75	81	85	89	91	92	91	88	83	77
	pm	48	48	53	59	62	68	69	66	68	64	58	51

Vancouver

	J	F	M	A	M	J	J	A	S	O	N	D
Temperature °F Max	41	44	50	58	64	69	74	73	65	57	48	43
Min	32	34	37	40	46	52	54	54	49	54	39	35
Temperature °C Max	5	7	10	14	18	21	23	23	18	14	9	6
Min	0	1	3	4	8	11	12	12	9	7	4	2
Humidity % am	93	91	91	89	88	87	89	90	92	92	91	91
pm	85	78	70	67	63	65	62	62	72	80	84	88

Vienna

	J	F	M	A	M	J	J	A	S	O	N	D
Temperature °F Max	34	38	47	58	67	73	76	75	68	56	45	37
Min	25	28	30	42	50	56	60	59	53	44	37	30
Temperature °C Max	1	3	8	15	19	23	25	24	20	14	7	3
Min	-4	-3	-1	6	10	14	15	15	11	7	3	-1
Humidity % am	81	80	78	72	74	74	74	78	83	86	84	84
pm	72	66	57	49	52	55	54	54	56	64	74	76

Warsaw

	J	F	M	A	M	J	J	A	S	O	N	D
Temperature °F	Max	32	32	42	53	67	73	75	73	66	55	42	35
	Min	22	21	28	37	48	54	58	56	49	41	33	28
Temperature °C	Max	0	0	6	13	19	23	24	23	19	14	6	3
	Min	-7	-6	-2	3	8	12	14	13	9	5	1	-2
Humidity %	am	83	82	83	83	79	82	84	88	90	89	90	86
	pm	74	71	64	59	55	60	63	63	63	67	78	78

Zurich

	J	F	M	A	M	J	J	A	S	O	N	D
Temperature °F	Max	36	41	51	59	67	73	76	75	69	57	45	37
	Min	26	28	34	40	47	53	56	56	51	43	35	29
Temperature °C	Max	2	5	10	15	19	23	25	24	20	14	7	3
	Min	-3	-2	1	4	8	12	14	13	11	6	2	-2
Humidity %	am	88	88	86	80	80	81	81	85	90	92	90	89
	pm	74	65	55	51	52	52	52	53	57	64	73	76